FRAMING
ROOFS

FROM THE EDITORS OF **Fine Homebuilding**®

The Taunton Press

The Taunton Press, Inc., 63 South Main Street, PO Box 5506, Newtown, CT 06470-5506
e-mail: tp@taunton.com

DESIGN AND LAYOUT: Cathy Cassidy

COVER PHOTOGRAPHERS: Front cover by Larry Hammerness. Back cover: (top left) by Susan Kahn, (top right) by Scott Gibson, courtesy of *Fine Homebuilding*, © The Taunton Press, Inc., (bottom left) by Charles Miller, courtesy *Fine Homebuilding*, © The Taunton Press, Inc., (bottom right) by Roe A. Osborn, courtesy of *Fine Homebuilding*, © The Taunton Press, Inc.

Library of Congress Cataloging-in-Publication Data
Framing roofs / from the editors of Fine homebuilding.
     p. cm. -- (For pros, by pros)
Includes index.
 ISBN-13: 978-1-56158-538-0
 ISBN-10: 1-56158-538-6
 1. Roofs--Design and construction. 2. Framing (Building) I. Fine
homebuilding. II. Series.
TH2393 .F727 2002
695--dc21
                    2002151272
Printed in the United States of America
10 9 8

Fine Homebuilding® is a trademark of The Taunton Press, Inc., registered in the U.S. Patent and Trademark Office

The following manufacturers/names appearing in *Framing Roofs* are trademarked: Bass Ale®, Calculated Industries®, Inc., Construction Master®, Linear Link®, Makita®, Minwax®, Pozzi®, Skil®, The Swanson® Tool Co.

Special thanks to the authors, editors, art directors,

copy editors, and other staff members of *Fine Homebuilding*

who contributed to the development of the articles in this book.

CONTENTS

PART 3: TRUSSES

INTRODUCTION

As a carpenter I came of age in the Midwest, where shallow roof pitches were as common as cornfields. When I finally got the chance to frame a steep roof, I got to frame it twice.

The first time, my fellow carpenters and I gave in to the lure of Friday quitting time—the promise of paychecks, cold beers, and two days off—and we failed to brace the roof properly. A big storm blew in that weekend and folded up the roof like someone snapping shut a set of Venetian blinds. It was a somber crew that assembled around the splintered mess on Monday morning.

Roofs are the most complicated and dangerous part of house framing. Geometry makes them complicated and height makes them dangerous. But roof framing is also pretty exciting. With the roof complete, you can stand back for the first time and see the building as the designer imagined it. And of course, framing a roof opens an umbrella over the house, protecting its vulnerable parts from the weather.

It's no wonder that finishing a roof frame is a traditional point of celebration. The "topping-out" ceremony is usually marked by nailing an evergreen bough to the highest part of the frame.

You won't find any advice on "topping-out" in this book. But you will find advice to help you deal with the complexities and dangers of roof framing. Written by builders from all over the country, the articles in this book were originally published in *Fine Homebuilding* magazine. If I had read these articles 20 years ago, that roof might never have blown over.

—Kevin Ireton,
editor-in-chief, *Fine Homebuilding*

A Different Approach to Rafter Layout

■ BY JOHN CARROLL

Earlier this year, I helped my friend Steve build a 12-ft. by 16-ft. addition to his house. A few days before we got to the roof frame, I arrived at his place with a rafter jig that I'd made on a previous job. I'm a real believer in the efficiency of this jig, so I told Steve that it would enable me to lay out the rafters for his addition in 10 minutes.

His look suggested that I had already fallen off one too many roofs. "Come on, John," he said. "Ten minutes?" I bet him a six-pack of imported beer, winner's choice, that I could do it.

Like most builders, I have a long and painful history of underestimating the time different jobs require. In this case, however, I was so certain that I agreed to all of Steve's conditions. In the allotted time, I would measure the span of the addition; calculate the exact height that the ridge should be set; measure and mark the plumb cut and the bird's mouth on the first rafter; and lay out the tail of the rafter to shape the eaves.

When the moment of reckoning arrived, we set a watch, and I went to work. Eight minutes later, I was done and in the process

secured the easiest six bottles of Bass Ale® in my life. With this layout in hand, we framed the roof in 5½ hours.

Why Should It Take an Hour to Do a 10-Minute Job?

That evening, as we enjoyed my beer, Steve's wife asked him how long he would have taken to do the same layout. "An hour," he said, "at least." Steve is a seasoned carpenter who now earns a living as a designer and construction manager. So why does a 10-minute job require 60, or possibly 90, minutes of his time? The answer is that Steve, like many builders, is confused by the process.

The first framing crew I worked with simply scaled the elevation of the ridge from

Laying out rafters doesn't need to be complicated or time-consuming. Using a jig makes the process quick and easy.

Rafter jig doubles as a cutting guide. Scaled to the 12-in-12 roof pitch, and with a 1x3 fence nailed to both sides of one edge, this plywood jig is used to lay out plumb and level cuts on the rafters. Notice that the fence is cut short to make room for the circular saw to pass by when the jig is used as a cutting guide. The jig will be used later to lay out plywood for the gable-end sheathing.

> *If you've always been vexed by roof framing, you may find my way easier to understand than most.*

the blueprint and then installed the ridge at that height. Once the ridge was set, they held the rafter board so that it ran past both the ridge and the top plate of the wall, then scribed the top and bottom cuts. Then they used this first rafter as a pattern for the rest. This technique worked. And because it's so simple and graphic, I'm convinced that it still is a widespread practice.

There are several reasons why I retired this method decades ago. To begin with, I haven't always had a drawing with an elevation of the roof system, which means that I couldn't always scale the height of the ridge. Second, it's just about impossible to scale the ridge with any degree of precision. Because of this fact, these roofs usually end up merely close to the desired pitch. Third, this method typically leaves the layout and cutting of the rafter tail for later, after the rafters are installed.

My technique is also different from the traditional approach espoused in most carpentry textbooks, which I've always found to be obscure and confusing. In rafter-length manuals and in booklets that come with rafter squares, dimensions are generally given in feet, inches, and fractions of inches. I use inches only and convert to decimals for my calculations. To convert a fraction to a decimal, divide the numerator (the top number) by the denominator (the bottom number). To convert a decimal to sixteenths, multiply the decimal by 16 and round to the nearest whole number. That number is the number of sixteenths.

Another difference in my approach is the measuring line I use. As the drawing on the facing page shows, the measuring line I employ runs along the bottom edge of the rafter. In contrast, most rafter-length manuals use a theoretical measuring line that runs from the top outside corner of the bearing wall to a point in the center of the ridge. A final thing that I do differently is use a site-built jig instead of a square to lay out the cuts on the rafter.

There are lots of ways to lay out rafters, but if you've always been vexed by roof framing, I think you'll find my way easier to understand than most.

Run and Roof Pitch Determine the Measuring Triangle

Framing a roof can be a little intimidating. Not only are you leaving behind the simple and familiar rectangle of the building, but you're starting a job where there is a disconcerting lack of tangible surfaces to measure from and mark on. Most of this job is done in midair. So where do you start?

Use the Measuring Triangle to Find the Rafter Length

1. Find the base of the measuring triangle (the run of the roof). Measure between bearing walls and subtract width of ridge, then divide by 2. (271 – 1.75 = 269.25; 269.25 ÷ 2 = 134.63).

2. Find the altitude of the measuring triangle (ridge height). Divide the base of the measuring triangle by 12 and multiply the result by the rise of the roof pitch. For a 12-in-12 pitch, the base and the altitude are the same. (134.63 in. ÷ 12 = 11.22; 11.22 x 12 = 134.63). (Editor's note: To present a set of consistent figures, we rounded to 134.63.)

3. Find the hypotenuse (rafter length). Divide the base of the triangle by 12 and multiply the result by the hypotenuse of the roof pitch, which is listed as length of common rafter on the rafter square (photo, p. 11). (134.63 in. ÷ 12 = 11.22; 11.22 x 16.97 = 190.40).

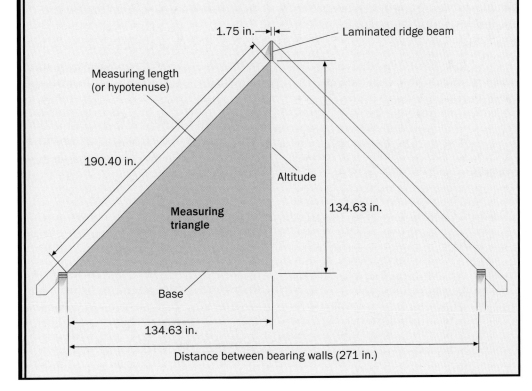

1.75 in. — Laminated ridge beam

Measuring length (or hypotenuse)

190.40 in.

Altitude

Measuring triangle

134.63 in.

Base

134.63 in.

Distance between bearing walls (271 in.)

There are only two things you need to lay out a gable roof— a choice of pitch and a measurement.

There are only two things you need to lay out a gable roof. One is a choice of pitch, and the other is a measurement. Usually the choice of pitch was made before the foundation was poured. The measurement is the distance between the bearing walls (drawing, p. 7).

After taking this measurement, deducting the thickness of the ridge, and dividing the remainder in half, you have the key dimension for laying out the rafters. This dimension could be called the "run" of the rafter; but because it is slightly different from what is called the run in traditional rafter layout, I'll use a different term. I'll call it the base of the measuring triangle. The measuring triangle is a concept that I use to calculate both the correct height of the ridge and the proper distance between the top and bottom cuts of the rafter, which I call the measuring length.

Working with this measuring triangle takes a little getting used to. The biggest problem is that when you start the roof layout, only one-third of the measuring triangle exists. As we've just seen, you find the base of the measuring triangle by measuring existing conditions. Then you create the altitude and the hypotenuse (same as the measuring length) by using that base and some simple arithmetic.

To see how this works, let's look at the steps I followed to frame the roof of a 12-ft. by 24-ft. addition I recently finished.

Build the Rafter Jig First

While the rest of the crew finished nailing down the second-floor decking, I began fabricating a rafter jig based on the pitch of the roof (left photo, p. 6). The desired pitch was 12-in-12 (the roof rises 12 in. vertically for every 12 in. of run horizontally). The basic design of this jig was simple, and the cost was reasonable: three scraps of wood and 10 minutes of time.

The first step in making this jig was finding a scrap of plywood about 30 in. wide, preferably with a factory-cut corner. Next, I measured and marked 24 in. out and 24 in. up from the corner to form a triangle. After connecting these marks with a straight line, I made a second line, parallel to and about 2½ in. above the first—the 1x3 fence goes between the lines—then cut the triangular-shaped piece along this second line. To finish the jig, I attached a 1x3 fence on both sides of the plywood between these two lines. I cut the fence short so that it didn't run all the way to the top on one side. That allowed me also to use the plywood as a cutting jig running my circular saw along one edge without the motor hitting the fence and offsetting the cut (right photo, p. 6).

Here I should pause and note an important principle. The jig was based on a 12-in-12 pitch, but because I wanted a larger jig, I simply multiplied both the rise and run figures by the same number—two—to get the 24-in. measurement. This way, I enlarged the jig without changing the pitch. This principle holds true for all triangles. Multiply all three sides by the same number to enlarge any triangle without changing its proportions, its shape, or its angles.

To use this jig, I hold the fence against the top edge of the rafter and scribe along the vertical edge of the plywood jig to mark plumb lines and along the horizontal edge to mark level lines.

There are at least four reasons why I go to the trouble to make this jig. First, I find it easier to visualize the cuts with the jig than with any of the manufactured squares made for this purpose. Second, identical layouts for both the top (ridge) and bottom (eave) cuts can be made in rapid succession. Third, I use the plumb edge as a cutting guide for my circular saw. Finally, I use the jig again when I'm framing and sheathing the gable end, finishing the eaves and rake, and installing siding on the gable. I also save the jig for future projects.

Step One: Determine the Base of the Measuring Triangle

The base of the measuring triangle is the key dimension for roof layout. In my system, the base of the triangle extends from the inside edge of the bearing wall to a point directly below the face of the ridge. In this addition, the distance between the bearing walls was 271 in. So to get the base of the measuring triangle, I subtracted the thickness of the ridge from 271 in. and divided the remainder by 2. Because the ridge was 1¾-in.-thick laminated beam, the base of the measuring triangle turned out to be 134.63 in. (271 − 1.75 = 269.25; 269.25 ÷ 2 = 134.63).

Step Two: Determine the Altitude of the Measuring Triangle

With the base of the measuring triangle in hand, it was easy to determine both the altitude and the hypotenuse. The altitude of this measuring triangle was, in fact, too easy to be useful as an example. Because we wanted to build a roof with a 12-in-12 pitch, the altitude had to be the same number as the base, or 134.63 in.

Let's pretend for a moment that I wanted a slightly steeper roof, one that had a 14-in-12 pitch. In a 14-in-12 roof, there are 14 in. of altitude for every 12 in. of base. To get the altitude of the measuring triangle, then, I would find out how many 12-in. increments there are in the base, then multiply that number by 14. In other words, divide 134.63 by 12, then multiply the result by 14. Here's what the math would look like: 134.63 in. ÷ 12 = 11.22; 11.22 x 14 = 157.08 in. Wouldn't it be nice if finding the hypotenuse of the measuring triangle was so simple? It is.

Step Three: Determine the Hypotenuse of the Measuring Triangle

Now let's return to our 12-in-12 roof. The base and the altitude of the measuring triangle are both 134.63 in. But what's the hypotenuse? One way to solve the problem of finding the hypotenuse is to use the Pythagorean theorem: $A^2 + B^2 = C^2$ (where A and B are the legs of the triangle and C is the hypotenuse).

There are other ways to solve this problem—with a construction calculator, with rafter manuals, with trigonometry— but I usually use the principle mentioned in step one. According to this principle, you can expand a triangle without changing the angles by multiplying all three sides by the same number.

The base of the measuring triangle is the key dimension for roof layout.

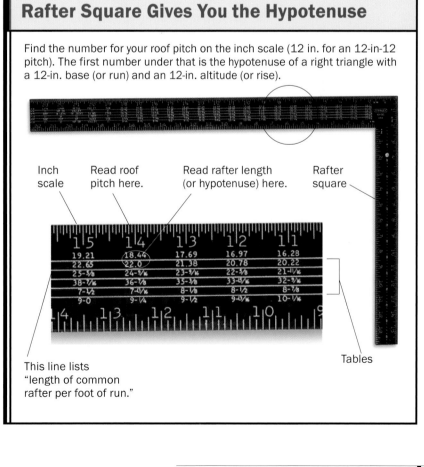

Rafter Square Gives You the Hypotenuse

Find the number for your roof pitch on the inch scale (12 in. for an 12-in-12 pitch). The first number under that is the hypotenuse of a right triangle with a 12-in. base (or run) and an 12-in. altitude (or rise).

Inch scale

Read roof pitch here.

Read rafter length (or hypotenuse) here.

Rafter square

Tables

This line lists "length of common rafter per foot of run."

For more than a century, carpenters have used the rafter tables stamped on rafter squares. The common table shows the basic proportions of triangles for 17 different pitches (photo, p. 9).

The base of all these triangles is 12; the altitude is represented by the number in the inch scale above the table. And the hypotenuse is the entry in the table. Under the number 12, for example, the entry is 16.97. This is the hypotenuse of a right triangle with a base and an altitude of 12.

To use this information to create the larger measuring triangle I needed for this roof, I simply multiplied the altitude and the hypotenuse by 11.22. This, you may recall, was the number I obtained in step two when I divided the base, 134.63 in., by 12. Now multiply the altitude and the hypotenuse of the small triangle by 11.22: 11.22 x 12 gives us an altitude of 134.63 in.; and 11.22 x 16.97 gives us a hypotenuse of 190.40 in.

So here is the technique I use for any gable roof. I find the base of the measuring triangle, divide it by 12, and multiply the result by the rise of the pitch to get the altitude of the measuring triangle (which determines the height to the bottom of the ridge). To get the hypotenuse, I divide the base of the triangle by 12 and multiply that by the hypotenuse of the pitch, which is found in the common rafter table.

Say the roof has an 8-in-12 pitch with a base of 134.63. I divide that number by 12 to get 11.22, then multiply that by 8 to get the ridge height of 89.76 in. To get the length of the rafter, I multiply 11.22 by 14.42 (the number found under the 8-in. notation on the rafter table), for a length between ridge and bearing wall of 161.79 in.

The only time I waver from this routine is when a bird's mouth cut the full depth of the wall leaves too little wood to support the eaves. How little is too little depends on the width of the rafter and the depth of the eave overhang, but I generally like to have at least 3 in. of uncut rafter running over the

bird's mouth. If I have too little wood, I let the bottom edge of the rafter land on top of the wall rather than aligning with the wall's inside edge. Then I determine how far the rafter will sit out from the inside edge of the bearing wall and use that inside point as the start of my measuring triangle.

Step Four: Setting the Ridge

I determined that the altitude of the measuring triangle was 134.63 in. This meant that the correct height to the bottom of the ridge was 134⅝ in. above the top plate of the wall. (Note: I usually hold the ridge board flush to the bottom of the rafter's plumb cut rather than the top.) To set the ridge at this height, we cut two posts, centered them between the bearing walls and braced them plumb. Before we installed the posts, we fastened scraps of wood to them that ran about 10 in. above their tops. Then, when we set the ridge on top of the posts (photo, facing page), we nailed through the scrap into the ridge. We placed one post against the existing house and the other about 10 in. inside the gable end of the addition. This kept it out of the way later when I framed the gable wall.

Getting the ridge perfectly centered is not as important as getting it the right height. If opposing rafters are cut the same length and installed identically, they will center the ridge.

Step Five: Laying Out the Main Part of the Rafter

I calculated a measuring length (or hypotenuse) for the rafter of 190.40 in., then used the jig as a cutting guide and made the plumb cut. I measured 190⅜ in. (converted from 190.40 in.) from the heel of the plumb cut and marked along the bottom of the rafter. Rather than have another carpenter

Setting the ridge. Temporary posts are set up to hold the ridge at the right height. The posts are braced 2x4s with a 2x4 scrap nailed to the top that rises 10 in. above the top of the post. The ridge is set on top of the post and nailed to the scrap of wood.

A clamped square serves as an extra pair of hands. It's easy to measure along the bottom of the rafter if you clamp a square to the bottom of the plumb cut and run your tape from there.

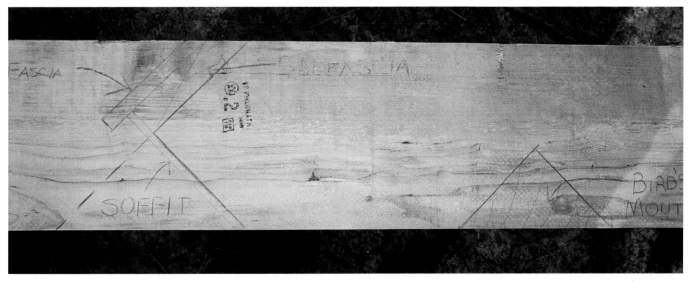

Visualizing the bird's mouth and rafter tail. Red lines on this marked-up rafter show where cuts will be made for the bird's mouth, at right, and rafter tail, at left. To determine the correct cut for the tail, the author marked out the subfascia, soffit, and fascia board.

hold the end of the tape, I usually clamp a square across the heel of the plumb cut, then pull the tape from the edge of the square (photo, facing page) to determine where the bird's mouth will be.

Once I marked where the bird's mouth would be, I used the jig to mark a level line out from the mark. This would be the heel cut, or the portion of the rafter that sits on top of the bearing wall.

After scribing a level line, I measured in the thickness of the wall, which was 5½ in., and marked. I slid the jig into place and scribed along the plumb edge from the mark to the bottom edge of the rafter. This completed the bird's mouth and, thus, the layout for the main portion of the rafter.

Step Six: Lay Out the Rafter Tail

The eaves on the existing house measure 16 in. out from the exterior wall, which meant I would make the eaves on the addition 16 in. wide. To lay out the rafter tail, I started with the finished dimension of 16 in. and then drew in the parts of the structure as I envisioned it (photo, above). In this

way, I worked my way back to the correct rafter-tail layout.

I began by holding the jig even with the plumb line of the bird's mouth. With the jig in this position, I measured and marked 16 in. from the corner along the level edge. Then I slid the jig down to this mark and scribed a vertical line. This line represented the outside of the fascia. Next I drew in a 1x6 fascia and a 2x subfascia. I also drew in the ⅜-in. soffit I would use. This showed me where to make the level line on the bottom of the rafter tail.

Step Seven: Preserve the Layout

The only dimension for this layout that I had to remember was 190⅜ in., the hypotenuse of the triangle and the measuring length of the rafter. I wrote the number where I could see it as I worked. To preserve the other three critical dimensions—one for the plumb cut of the bird's mouth and the other two for the rafter tail—I used the rafter jig to extend reference points to the bottom edge of the rafter; then I transferred these marks to a strip of wood, or measuring stick (photo, p. 14). I was ready to begin cutting the rafters.

Marking the bird's mouth and tail. Once the start of the heel cut was determined by measuring from the bottom of the plumb cut, this measuring stick was used to transfer the dimensions of the bird's mouth and rafter tail. The cutting lines were marked using the rafter jig.

Step Eight: Marking and Cutting the Rafters

Some carpenters lay out and cut one rafter, then use it as a pattern for the rest, and I'll often do that on a smaller roof. On this roof, where the rafters were made of 20-ft. long 2x10s and where I was laying them out by myself, this method would have meant a lot of heavy, awkward, unnecessary work. In-

stead of using a 100-lb. rafter as a template, I used my jig, my tape measure, and the measuring stick.

Moving to the end of the 2x12, I clamped the jig in place and made the plumb cut. (The steep pitch of this roof made clamping the jig a good idea. Usually, I just hold it to the rafter's edge the way you would when using a framing square as a cutting guide.) Then I clamped my square across the heel of that cut, pulled a 190⅝-in. measurement from that point, and marked along the bot-

tom edge of the board. Next I aligned the first mark on the measuring stick with the 190⅜-in. mark and transferred the other three marks on the measuring stick to the bottom edge of the rafter (photo, facing page).

To finish the layout, I used the jig to mark the level and plumb lines of the bird's mouth and the rafter tail (photo, above). For all four of these lines, I kept the jig in the same position and simply slid it up or down the rafter until either the plumb or level edge engaged the reference mark. It was quick and easy.

The two cuts that formed the rafter tail were simple, straight cuts that I made with my circular saw. To cut the bird's mouth, I cut as far as I could with my circular saw without overcutting, then finished the cut with my jigsaw.

John Carroll is a contributing editor to Fine Home-building and the author of Measuring, Marking and Layout: A Guide for Builders and Working Alone, published by The Taunton Press.

Framing a Gable Roof

■ BY LARRY HAUN

One of my earliest and fondest memories dates from the 1930s. I remember watching a carpenter laying out rafters, cutting them with a handsaw, and then over the next several days, artfully and precisely constructing a gable roof. His work had a fascinating, almost Zen-like quality to it. In a hundred imperceptible ways, the roof became an extension of the man.

But times change, and the roof that took that carpenter days to build now takes pieceworkers (craftspersons who get paid by the piece and not by the hour) a matter of hours. Since they first appeared on job sites, pieceworkers have given us new tools, ingenious new methods of construction, and many efficient shortcuts. But what skilled pieceworkers haven't done is sacrifice sound construction principles for the sake of increased production. Quite the opposite is true; they've developed solid construction procedures that allow them to keep up with demand, yet still construct a well-built home.

The secret to successful piecework, from hanging doors to framing roofs, is to break down a process into a series of simple steps. To demonstrate just how easy roof framing can be (with a little practice), I'll describe how to cut and stack a gable roof the way pieceworkers do it.

The Rafter Horse

To begin with, pieceworkers try to avoid cutting one piece at a time. They'll build a pair of simple horses out of 2x stock so that they can stack the rafters on edge and mark and cut them all at once. To build the rafter horses, lay four 3-ft. long 2x6s flat and nail a pair of 2x blocks onto each, with a 1½ in. gap between them so that you can slip in a long 2x6 or 2x8 on edge (bottom photo, facing page). An alternate method is to cut a notch 1½ in. wide by about 4 in. deep into four scraps of 4x12. Then you can slip a long 2x6 or 2x8 on edge into these notches. Either of these horses can easily be broken down and carried from job to job. The horses hold the rafters off the ground, providing plenty of clearance for cutting.

Cutting the Rafters

Rafters can be cut using a standard 7¼-in. sidewinder or worm-drive circular saw. This isn't the first choice for most pieceworkers, who prefer to use more specialized tools

The key to production roof framing is to minimize wasted motion. Here, carpenters nail gable studs plumb by eye—there's no need to lay out the top plates. The next step is to snap a line across the rafter tails and cut the tails off with a circular saw.

Pieceworkers typically build a pair of simple portable rafter horses. The horses allow them to stack rafters off the ground on edge so that they can mark and cut the rafters all at once.

TIP

If you are using a standard circular saw, load rafter stock on the horses with their crowns, or convex edges, facing up—same as the rafters will be oriented in the roof frame.

One way to lay out rafters is with a site-built rafter tee. The fence on top of the tee allows easy scribing of the ridge cuts and birds' mouths. When laid out this way, rafters are cut one at a time with a circular saw.

(especially when cutting simple gable roofs). But it is the more affordable choice for most custom-home builders. If you are using a standard circular saw, load rafter stock on the horses with their crowns, or convex edges, facing up—same as the rafters will be oriented in the roof frame.

Determine which end of the stack will receive the plumb cuts for the ridge and flush this end. An easy way to do this is to hold a stud against the ends and pull all the rafters up against it. Then measure down from this end on the two outside rafters in the stack and make a mark corresponding to the heel cut of the bird's mouth (the notch in the rafter that fits over the top plate and consists of a plumb heel cut and a level seat cut). Snap a line across the tops of the rafters to connect the marks.

Next, make a rafter pattern, or layout tee, for scribing the ridge cuts and birds' mouths (photo, above). I usually start with a 2-ft. long 1x the same width as the rafters. Using a triangular square such as a Speed Square from The Swanson® Tool Co., scribe the ridge cut at one end of the template. Then move down the template about one foot and scribe the heel cut of the bird's mouth, transferring this line across the top edge of

the template. This will serve as your registration mark when laying out the birds' mouths.

The layout of the bird's mouth on the tee depends on the size of the rafters. For 2x4 rafters, which are still used occasionally around here, measure 2½ in. down the plumb line and scribe the seat cut of the bird's mouth perpendicular to the plumb line. Leaving 2½ in. of stock above the plate ensures a strong rafter tail on 2x4 rafter stock. One drawback to this is that for roof pitches greater than 4-in-12, 2x4 rafters will have less than a 3½-in.-long seat cut. Consequently, the rafters won't have full bearing on a 2x4 top plate. However, this presents no problems structurally as long as the rafters are stacked, nailed, and blocked properly (the building code in Los Angeles requires a minimum bearing of 1½ in.). For 2x6 or larger rafters, you can make the seat cuts 3½ in. long without weakening the tails.

Once the layout tee is marked and cut, nail a 1x2 fence to the upper edge of the tee. This allows you to place the tee on a rafter and mark it quickly and accurately. Make sure you position the fence so that it won't keep you from seeing the ridge cut or your

To save time, ridges can be gang-cut with a 16-in. beam saw. Though these saws won't cut all the way through anything wider than a 2x4 at a 4-in-12 pitch, where necessary each cut can be completed using a standard circular saw.

registration mark. Use the layout tee to mark the ridge cut and bird's mouth on each rafter. Scribe all the ridges first at the flush ends of the stock, sliding the rafters over one at a time. Then do the same for the seat cuts, aligning the registration mark on the template with the chalk marks on the rafters.

Next with the rafters on edge, cut the ridges with your circular saw, again moving the rafters over one at a time. Then flip the rafters on their sides and make the seat cuts, overcutting just enough to remove the birds' mouths.

Production Rafter-Cutting

Cutting common rafters with production tools is both faster and easier than the method I've just described. In this case, you'll want to stack the rafters on edge, but with their crowns facing down. Flush up the rafters on one end and snap a chalkline across them about 3 in. down from the flush ends (the greater the roof pitch and rafter width, the greater this distance). The chalk-line corresponds to the short point of the

An alternate method is to use a Linear Link® saw, a Skil® worm-drive saw fitted with a bar and chain.

One method for gang-cutting birds' mouths is to cut the heels with a worm-drive saw (left) and the seats with a worm-drive saw fitted with a swing table, an accessory base that adjusts from –5° to 68° (right).

ridge plumb cut. Snap another line the appropriate distance (the common-rafter length) from this point to mark the heel cuts of the birds' mouths. Then measure back up from this mark about 2½ in. and snap a third line to mark the seat cut of the bird's mouth. This measurement will vary depending on the size of the rafters, the pitch of the roof, and the cutting capacity of your saw (more on that later).

Now gang-cut the ridge cuts using a beam saw (top photo, p. 19). Blocks nailed to the top of the rafter horses will help hold the stack upright. My 16-in. Makita® beam saw will cut through a 2x4 on edge at more than an 8-in-12 pitch and will saw most of the way through a 2x6 at a 4-in-12 pitch. To determine the angle at which to set your

saw, use a calculator with a tangent key or, just as easy, look up the angle in your rafter-table book.

For steeper pitches or wider stock, make a single pass with the beam saw (or a standard circular saw) and then finish each cut with a standard circular saw, moving the rafters over one at a time. This way the only mark needed is the chalkline. The kerf from the first cut will accurately guide the second cut.

To make the process go even faster, apply paraffin to the sawblade and shoe. Also try to stay close to your power source. If you have to roll out 100 ft. of cord or more, the saw will lose some power and won't operate at its maximum efficiency.

Another method for cutting ridges is to use the Linear Link model VCS-12 saw. The model CS-12 is a Skil worm-drive saw fitted with a bar and cutting chain that lets the saw cut to a depth of 12 in. at 90°. It's adjustable to cut angles up to 45°. You can buy the saw or a conversion kit that will fit any Skil worm drive.

With the right tools, the birds' mouths can also be gang-cut with the rafters on edge. Gang-cutting birds' mouths works

especially well because you needn't overcut the heel or the seat cut, which weakens the tail. For the heel cuts, set your worm-drive saw to the same angle as the ridge cut and to the proper depth, and then make a single cut across all the rafters (left photo, facing page).

Seat cuts are made using a 7¼-in. or, better yet, 8¼-in worm-drive saw fitted with a swing table. A swing table replaces the saw's standard saw base and allows the saw to be tilted to angles up to 68° (right photo, facing page). I bought mine from Pairis Enterprises and Manufacturing. Set the swing table to 90° minus the plumb-cut angle (for example, 63½° for a 6-in-12 roof) and make the seat cuts, again in one pass.

The only drawback to using a swing table with a worm-drive saw is that it won't allow a substantial depth of cut at sharp angles, so

A dado kit enables you to make birds' mouth cuts in a single pass. Unfortunately, this worm-drive saw accessory is no longer available, but used kits can sometimes be found.

it limits the amount of bearing that the rafters will have on the top plates (about 2½ in. maximum with an 8¼-in saw). Again, this is of little concern if the roof is framed properly. Nevertheless, for jobs requiring a greater depth of cut, Pairis Enterprises has a swing table to fit 16-in. Makita® beam saws.

Another way to gang-cut birds' mouths is to use a special dado kit that mounts on a worm-drive saw. As shown in the photo on p. 21, this stack-type dado can make up to a 3¼-in.-wide seat cut in a single pass. Unfortunately, the kit is no longer available, but I still see these dado sets in use on job sites. Once you get used to working with these production tools, you'll find that it takes longer to stack the rafters than to cut them.

With the rafters cut, you can now carry them over to the house and lean them against the walls, ridge-end up. The rafter tails will be cut to length in place later.

Staging and Layout

Now it's time to prepare a sturdy platform from which to frame the roof. The easiest way is to simply tack 1x6s or strips of plywood across the joists below the ridge line to create a catwalk (the joists are usually installed before the roof framing begins). Run this catwalk the full length of the building. If the ridge works out to be higher than about 6 ft., pieceworkers will usually frame and brace the bare bones of the roof off the catwalk and then install the rest of the rafters while walking the ridge.

For added convenience, most roof stackers install a hook on their worm-drive saws that allows them to hang their saw from a joist or rafter. When not in use, the hook folds back against the saw and out of the way.

The next step is to lay out the ridge. Most codes require the ridge to be one size larger than the rafters to ensure proper bearing (2x4 rafters require a 1x6 or 2x6 ridge). Make sure to use straight stock for the ridge. In the likely event that more than one ridge

board is required to run the length of the building, cut the boards to length so that each joint falls in the center of a rafter pair. The rafters will then help to hold the ridge together. Let the last ridge board run long—it will be cut to length after the roof is assembled.

Be sure to align the layout of the ridge to that of the joists so that the rafters and joists will tie together at the plate line. If the rafters and joists are both spaced 16 in. o. c., each rafter will tie into a joist. If the joists are spaced 16 in. o. c. and the rafters 24 in. o. c., then a rafter will tie into every fourth joist. Regardless, no layout is necessary on the top plates for the rafters. Rafters will either fall next to a joist or be spaced the proper distance apart by frieze blocks installed between them. Once the ridge is marked and cut, lay the boards end to end on top of the catwalk.

Nailing It Up

Installation of the roof can be accomplished easily by two carpenters. The first step is to pull up a rafter at the gable end. While one carpenter holds up the rafter at the ridge, the other toenails the bottom end of the rafter to the plate with two 16d nails on one side and one 16d nail (or backnail) on the other. The process is repeated with the opposing rafter. The two rafters meet in the middle and hold each other up temporarily, unless, of course, you're framing in a Wyoming wind. If that's the case, nail a temporary 1x brace diagonally from the rafters to a joist.

Next, move to the opposite end of the first ridge section and toenail another rafter pair in the same way. Now reach down and pull up the ridge between the two rafter pairs. There is no need to predetermine the ridge height. Drive two nails straight through the ridge and into the end of the first rafter, then angle two more through the ridge into the opposing rafter. To keep from

Pieceworkers don't waste time predetermining the ridge height. Instead, they toenail a pair of rafters to the top plates at either end of the ridge board, then raise the ridge board between the rafters and nail the rafters to it with 16d nails. A 2x4 sway brace is installed before the intermediate rafters are nailed up.

dulling a sawblade when you're sheathing the roof, avoid nailing into the top edge of a rafter. At this point, nail a 2x4 leg to the ridge board at both ends to give it extra support. If these legs need to be cut to two different lengths to fit beneath the ridge, it means that the walls probably aren't parallel and, consequently, that the ridge board isn't level. In this case yank the nails out of the rafter pair at the top plate on the high end of the ridge and slide out the rafters until the ridge is level. The key to avoiding all this

hassle is, of course, to make sure the walls are framed accurately in the first place.

Next, plumb this ridge section. This can be accomplished in a couple of ways. One way is to nail a 2x4 upright to the gable end ahead of time so that it extends up to the height of the ridge. This allows you to push the end rafters against the upright and to install a 2x4 sway brace extending from the top plate to the ridge at a 45° angle. This is a permanent brace. Nail it in between the layout lines at the ridge.

Roof Framing Tips

Check your blueprints for the roof pitch, lengths of overhangs, rafter spacing, and size of the framing members. But don't rely on the blueprints to determine the span. Instead, measure the span at the top plates. Measure both ends of the building to make sure the walls are parallel; accurate wall framing is crucial to the success of production roof framing.

Once you've determined the length of the rafters, compensate for the thickness of the ridge by subtracting one half the ridge thickness from the length of the rafters. Though theoretically this reduction should be measured perpendicular to the ridge cut, in practice for roofs pitched 6-in-12 and under with 2x or smaller ridges, measuring along the edge of the rafters is close enough. For 2x ridge stock, that means subtracting ¾ in. from the rafter length. An alternative is to subtract the total thickness of the ridge from the span of the building before consulting your rafter book.

Once you've figured the common-rafter length, determine the number of common rafters you need. If the rafters are spaced 16 in. o. c., divide the length of the building in feet by four, multiply that figure by three, and then add one more. That will give you the number of rafters on each side of the roof. If there are barge rafters, add four more rafters. If the rafters are spaced 24 in. o. c., simply take the length of the building in feet and add two, again adding four more to the total if barge rafters are called for.

A second method is to use your eye as a gauge. Sighting down from the end of the ridge, align the outboard face of the end rafters with the outside edges of the top and bottom plates, and then nail up a sway brace. Either way, the ridge can be plumbed without using a level. This means carrying one less tool up with you when you stack the roof.

With the bare bones of the first ridge section completed, raise the remaining ridge sections in the same way, installing the minimum number of rafter pairs and support legs to hold them in place. When you reach the opposite end of the building, eyeball the last rafter pair plumb, scribe the end cut on the ridge (if the ridge is to be cut at the plate line), slide the rafters over a bit and cut the ridge to length with a circular saw. Then reposition the rafters and nail them to the ridge. Install another sway brace to stabilize the entire structure.

Now stack the remaining rafters, installing the frieze blocks as you go. Nail through the sides of the rafters into the blocks, using two 16d nails for up to 2x12 stock and three 16d nails for wider stock. Where a rafter falls next to a joist, drive three 16d nails through the rafter into the joist. This forms a rigid triangle that helps to tie the roof system together.

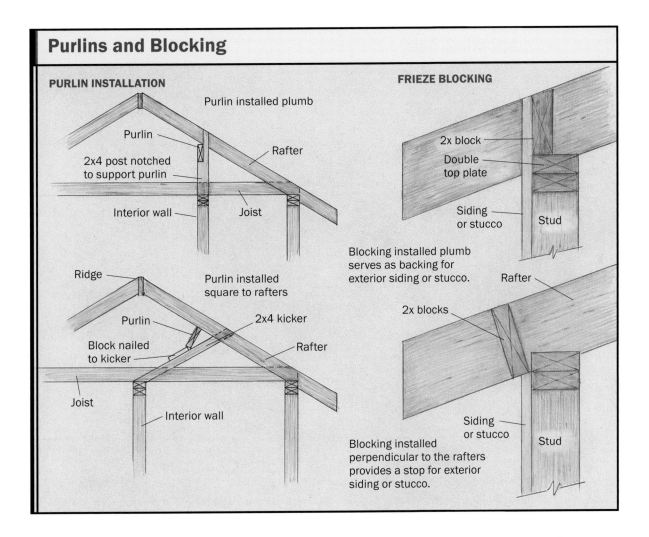

Purlins and Blocking

PURLIN INSTALLATION

Purlin installed plumb

Purlin

2x4 post notched
to support purlin

Rafter

Interior wall

Joist

Ridge

Purlin installed
square to rafters

Purlin

2x4 kicker

Block nailed
to kicker

Rafter

Joist

Interior wall

FRIEZE BLOCKING

2x block

Double
top plate

Siding
or stucco

Stud

Blocking installed plumb
serves as backing for
exterior siding or stucco.

Rafter

2x blocks

Siding
or stucco

Stud

Blocking installed
perpendicular to the rafters
provides a stop for exterior
siding or stucco.

Blocking a Gable Roof

In some parts of the country, blocking is not installed between the rafters at the plate. But in many areas, building codes require blocks. I think they're important. They stabilize the rafters, provide perimeter nailing for roof sheathing and tie the whole roof system together. They also provide backing or act as a stop for siding or stucco. If necessary, they can easily be drilled and screened for attic vents.

There are two methods for blocking a gable roof (drawings, above right). The first is to install the blocking plumb so that it lines up with the outside edge of the top plate, allowing the blocks to serve as backing for the exterior siding or stucco. This requires the blocking to be ripped narrower than the rafters. The other method is to install the blocking perpendicular to the rafters just outside the plate line. The blocking provides a stop for the siding or stucco, eliminating the need to fit either up between the rafters. Also, there's no need to rip the blocking with this method, which saves time. Either way, blocks are installed as the rafters are nailed up. Sometimes blocks need to be cut a bit short to fit right. Rafter thickness can vary from region to region (usually it's related to moisture content), so check your rafter stock carefully.

Collar Ties and Purlins

In some cases building codes require the use of collar ties to reinforce the roof structure or purlins to reduce the rafter span (drawings, above). Collar ties should be installed

TIP

In some parts of the country, rafters have to be tied to the top plates or blocking with framing anchors or hurricane ties for added security against earthquakes or high winds. Check your local codes.

Two Methods for Supporting Barge Rafters

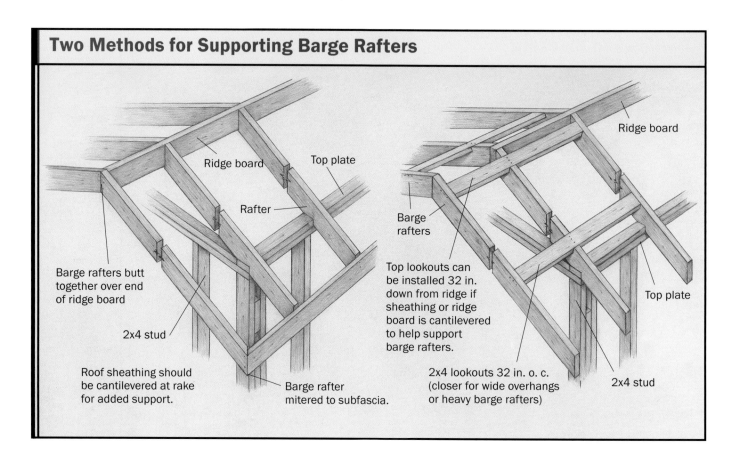

Ridge board

Top plate

Rafter

Barge rafters butt together over end of ridge board

2x4 stud

Roof sheathing should be cantilevered at rake for added support.

Barge rafter mitered to subfascia.

Ridge board

Barge rafters

Top lookouts can be installed 32 in. down from ridge if sheathing or ridge board is cantilevered to help support barge rafters.

Top plate

2x4 lookouts 32 in. o. c. (closer for wide overhangs or heavy barge rafters)

2x4 stud

The notches in the rake rafters are most easily cut when you're working at the rafter horses.

horizontally on the upper third of the rafter span. They're usually made of 1x4 or wider stock, placed every 4 ft. and secured with five 8d nails on each end so that they tie the opposing rafters together.

Purlins should be placed near the middle of the rafter span. They can be toenailed to the rafters either plumb or square. If there's an interior wall beneath the center of the rafter span, install the purlin plumb and directly over the wall. This makes it easy to support the purlin with several 2x4 posts that bear on the top plate of the interior wall. The 2x4s are notched so that they both support the purlin and are nailed to the sides of the rafters.

If there isn't a wall beneath the center of the rafter span, toenail the purlin square to the rafters and install 2x4 kickers up from the nearest parallel wall at an angle not exceeding 45°. A block nailed to each kicker below the purlin will hold the purlin in place. Kickers are typically installed every

4 ft. Large purlins such as 2x12s require fewer kickers.

In some parts of the country, rafters have to be tied to the top plates or blocking with framing anchors or hurricane ties for added security against earthquakes or high winds. Check your local codes.

Framing the Gable Ends

Gable ends are filled in with gable studs spaced 16 in. o. c. Place the two center studs (on either side of the ridge) 14 in. apart. This leaves enough room for a gable vent, which allows air to circulate in the attic. Measure the lengths of these two studs, then calculate the common difference of the gable studs, or the difference in length between successive studs. Then you can quickly determine the lengths of the remaining studs. A pocket calculator makes it easy.

For a 4-in-12 roof pitch, the equation goes like this: 4 ÷ 12 x 16 = 5.33. Four equals the rise, 12 the run and 16 the on-center spacing. The answer to the problem, 5.33, or 5⅜ in., is the common difference. Another way to calculate this is to divide the unit rise by three and add the answer and the unit rise together. For a 4-in-12 pitch, 4 ÷ 3 = 1.33 + 4 = 5.33. For the angle cuts, set your saw to the same angle as that of the plumb cut on the rafters. Cut four gable studs at each length, and you'll have all the gable studs you'll need for both gable ends.

Once the gable studs are cut, nail them plumb using your eye as a gauge. There is no need to lay out the top plates or to align the gable studs with the studs below. Be careful not to put a crown in the end rafters when you're nailing the gable studs in place.

Finishing the Overhangs

The next step is to install the *barge rafters* if the plans call for them; these are rafters that hang outside the building and help support the rake. Sometimes barge rafters are supported by the ridge, fascia, and roof sheathing. In this case, the ridge board extends beyond the building line so that the opposing barge rafters butt together over its end and are face nailed to it. At the bottoms the barge rafters are mitered to the subfascia boards, which also extend beyond the building line. The roof sheathing cantilevers out and is nailed to the tops of the barge rafters.

Another way to support barge rafters is with lookouts. A lookout is a 2x4 laid flat that butts against the first inboard rafter, passes through a notch cut in the end rafter, and cantilevers out to support the barge rafter (drawing, facing page). Lookouts are usually installed at the ridge, at the plate line and 32 in. o. c. in between (closer for wide overhangs or heavy barge rafters). If the roof sheathing cantilevers out over the eaves (adding extra support for the barge

rafters), then the top lookouts can be placed 32 in. down from the ridge.

The notches in the rake rafters are most easily cut when you're working at the rafter horses. Pick out four straight rafters and lay out the notches while you're laying out for the birds' mouths and ridge cuts. Cut these notches by first making two square crosscuts with a circular saw 1½ in. deep across the top edges of the rafters. Then turn the rafters on their sides and plunge cut the bottom of the notch.

Lookouts are cut to length after they're nailed up. Snap a line and cut them off with a circular saw. That done, the barge rafters are face nailed to the ends of the lookouts with 16d nails.

The final step in framing a gable roof is to snap a line across the rafter tails and cut them to length. Cutting the rafters in place ensures that the fascia will be straight. Use the layout tee or a bevel square to mark the plumb cut. If the rafters are cut square, use a triangular square. Then, while walking the plate or a temporary catwalk nailed to the rafter tails, lean over and cut off the tails with a circular saw.

Larry Haun has been building houses for over 50 years. He is the author of several carpentry books including, Habitat for Humanity How to Build a House, *published by The Taunton Press. His website is www.carpentryforeveryone.com.*

Sources

Big Foot Tools
4395 S. Cameron St. Ste A
Las Vegas, NV 89103
(702) 565-9954
www.bigfoottools.com
Swing table, head cutter

Muskegan Power Tool
2357 Whitehall Rd.
North Muskegan, MI 49445
(800) 635-5465
www.linearlink.com
Linear Link VCS-12 saw

Pairis Products
P.O. Box 292772
Phelan, CA 92329
(760) 868-0973
www.bestconstruction-tools.com

Swanson Tool Co.
211 Ontario St.
Frankfort, IL 60423
(800) 291-3471
www.swansontoolco.com

Framing a Hip Roof

■ BY LARRY HAUN

I built my first hip roof in 1951 while in the Navy being trained as a carpenter. I dutifully laid out my rafters by stepping them off with a framing square. When I was finished, the commons were fine, but the hips came out short. Ever since then, I've relied on a book of rafter tables to determine rafter lengths rather than trust my ability to count steps with a square. Having framed hip roofs for so many years, I'm surprised that so many carpenters seem reluctant to build hip roofs. Maybe they're afraid that the framing is too complicated or beyond their abilities. I think that once you've learned to frame a gable, cutting and building a hip roof requires few additional skills.

A hip roof has the advantage of being inherently stronger than a gable roof. The hip rafters act as braces in the roof to resist the destructive forces of earthquakes, and the roof sloping up from all four sides of a hip roof offers no flat ends to catch high winds. Another advantage to hip roofs is that changing the roof style from gable to hip can transform the appearance of a house, offering a nice variation from the gable roof.

A Hip Roof Begins with Common Rafters

Hip rafters extend from the corners of the building up to the ridge. On both sides of the hips, common rafters, called king commons, meet the ridge at the same point as the hips (drawing, p. 30). The side and end king commons and the hip rafters are the main framing components of the hip roof.

The end king common runs from the middle of the end wall to the ridge. This rafter is the same pitch as the rest of the roof, and it is the key to the hip roof's ending with a pitched plane instead of the more common vertical gable. The hip rafters form the line of intersection between the side-roof and end-roof planes. The first step in framing a hip roof is determining the span

Fitting together pieces of the hip-roof puzzle. If all of the rafters have been cut properly, assembling a hip roof should be a painless process. Here, the author lines up a jack rafter for nailing.

Anatomy of a Hip Roof

The hip rafters run at a 45° angle from the corners of the building to the ridge. These rafters are flanked with the side and end king commons, and the triangular spaces left are filled with jack rafters. Common rafters complete the framing down the length of the building. The total width of the building is the rafter span, and the distance from the outside of the building to the ridge is the run of the common rafters. The run also determines the position of the king commons.

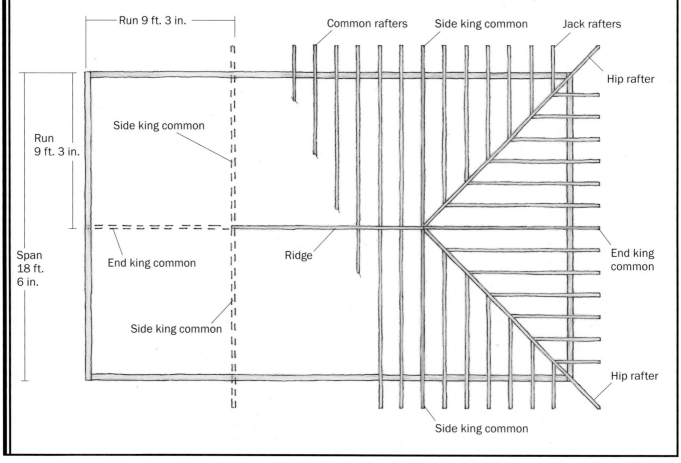

of the roof, which establishes the location of the king commons. The garage featured in the photos in this article is 18 ft. 6 in. wide. The end king common, which is at the exact center of the span, is 9 ft. 3 in. from the outside of the garage. This number also represents the run of the rafters. After marking the location of the end king commons, I measure down the sides of the building the same distance, and then I mark the position of the side king commons. Next I lay out the rafter locations on the double-wall plates.

Rafter Templates Streamline Measurement and Layout

The roof of our garage has a 4-in-12 pitch, which means that the common rafters rise 4 in. vertically for every 12 in. they run horizontally. Because hip rafters run at a 45° angle to their neighboring commons in plan view, hip rafters must run 17 in. for every 4 in. of rise. (By the way, 17 in. is the hypotenuse of a right triangle with 12-in. legs.)

When cutting rafters for any type of roof, especially a hip roof, rafter templates are a great way to speed the layout process. These neat little site-built aids have the rafter plumb cut on one end and the bird's mouth layout on the other. For this project I will need templates with pitches of 4-in-12 for the common rafters and 4-in-17 for the hips.

For the common-rafter template, I use a 2-ft.-long piece of 1x6, which is the same width as my rafter stock (sidebar, right). I place my rafter square, or triangle square, on the template stock, pivot it to the correct pitch number (4) on the row of numbers marked "common," and mark the ridge plumb cut along the pivot side. I then slide the square down the template about 1 ft. and make a second plumb mark for the heel cut of the bird's mouth. I square this line across the top edge of the template so that I can use the line as a reference when marking the rafters.

A level seat cut combines with the plumb heel cut to make up the bird's mouth of the rafter. The seat cut of the bird's mouth lands directly on the 2x4 top plate, so I make the seat cuts about 3½ in. long, squared off to the heel-cut line. The plumb distance from the seat cut of the bird's mouth to the top edge of the rafter is the height above plate and must be the same for both hip-rafter and common-rafter templates in order to maintain the plane of the roof sheathing. Hip rafters are cut out of stock that is 2 in. wider than the commons so that the jack rafters will have full bearing on the hip. The hip template is also cut out of wider stock, in this case 1x8. The ridge cut is laid out the same as for the common-rafter template except that the square is pivoted to 4 and 17 if you're using a framing square or 4 on the hip-valley index of a triangle square. Again, I move the square down the template about 1 ft. and scribe a second plumb mark for the heel cut, with the line squared across the top. Next, I mark off the height above plate on the heel plumb line of the hip template and scribe the level seat-cut line at a right angle from this point.

Templates Facilitate Rafter Layout

Making templates is easy with a triangle square. Line up the correct pitch number with the edge of the template stock to mark the ridge plumb cut and the heel cut of the bird's mouth. The seat cut is just wide enough to bear fully on the 2x4 top wall plate. The shaded area is waste (top). After the template is cut, a narrow fence is mounted on top for alignment with the rafter stock.

Two templates are necessary for hip-roof layout, the hip based on a 4-in-17 pitch (middle) and the common template set up on a 4-in-12 pitch (bottom). Each has a plumb cut on the ridge end and a bird's mouth on the other. A line squared across the top of the template is used as a reference to position the template on the rafters.

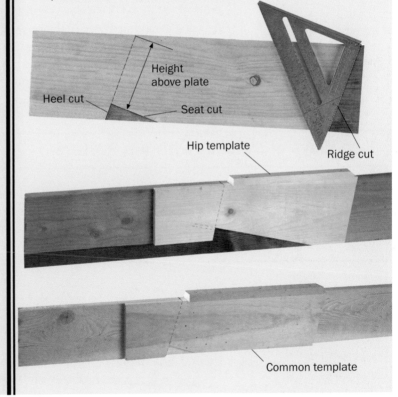

Height above plate

Heel cut

Seat cut

Hip template

Ridge cut

Common template

Lower Hip Rafters at the Seat Cut

The height above plate for the hip rafters is measured from the centerline of the rafter. Because the two roof planes intersect at an angle, the top edge of the hip rafter needs to be beveled slightly from the centerline to maintain the roof planes (drawing, below). This process of beveling a hip rafter (or a valley rafter) is known as backing.

A more efficient solution to this problem is lowering the hip rafter slightly (called "dropping the hip") by simply cutting the seat deeper. The size of the drop depends on the thickness of the rafter stock and the pitch of the roof. I determine this distance by using a framing square (right drawing, facing page). For this 4-in-12 pitch roof, I need to drop the hip about ¼ in.

I subtract that ¼ in. from the height above plate on my hip-rafter template and make a new level seat-cut line at this point. When my layouts are complete, I cut out the templates carefully to ensure their accuracy. After cutting the bird's mouth in the hip-rafter template, I rip the tail section to the same width as the common rafters, which allows the soffit material to be properly aligned. I finish the templates by nailing a 1x2 fence to the upper edge of the template.

The Quickest Way to Get Rafter Lengths Is from Tables

All of the information needed to calculate rafter lengths is right there on any framing square. But out here in southern California, I don't know of any framers who still use one for this purpose. Some framers determine rafter length using a feet-inch calcula-

---

Two Ways of Dealing with Hip Rafters

The problem. Without modification, the top edges of the hip rafter would be higher than the king commons.

Dropping the hip. The entire rafter can be lowered by deepening the seat cut. See right drawing, facing page.

Backing the hip. The top edge of the hip rafter can be beveled slightly from the centerline to the outer edge.

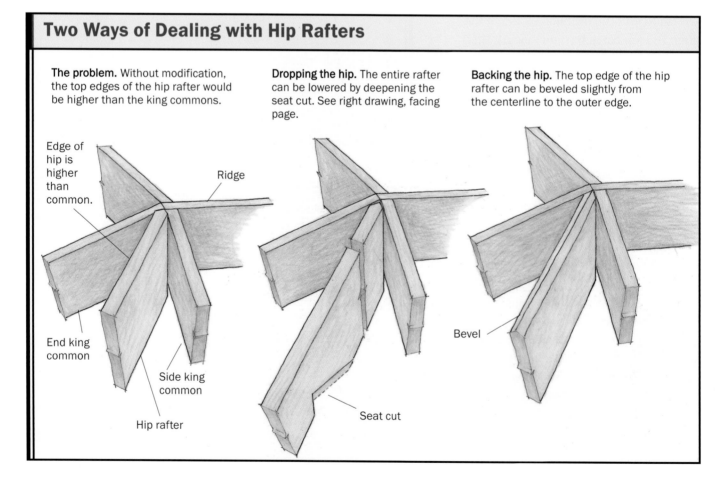

Edge of hip is higher than common.

Ridge

End king common

Side king common

Hip rafter

Seat cut

Bevel

The Hip-Rafter Ridge Cut

A double side cut on the ridge end of the hip rafter lets it fit nicely between the side and end king commons. To make this cut, scribe two parallel plumb-cut lines from the ridge end of the hip template 1½ in. apart. With the sawblade set at 45°, saw along both lines in opposite directions.

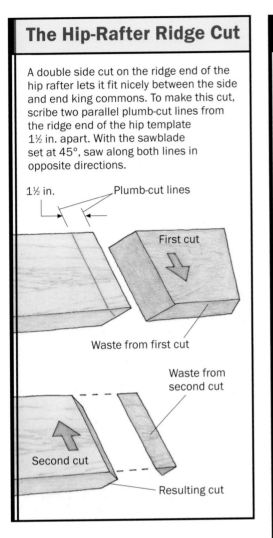

Finding the Hip-Rafter Drop

Hip rafters can be lowered slightly to put their edges in the same plane as the common rafters.

Step 1. Using a framing square, lay out a 4-in-17 pitch along the edge of any piece of rafter stock.

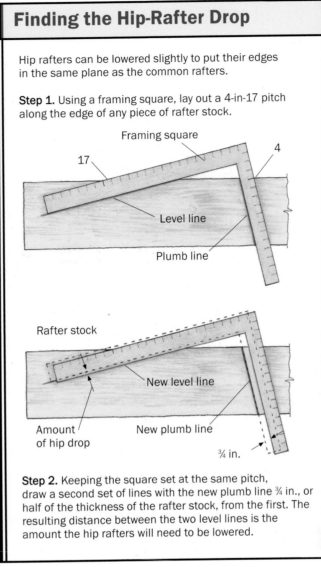

Step 2. Keeping the square set at the same pitch, draw a second set of lines with the new plumb line ¾ in., or half of the thickness of the rafter stock, from the first. The resulting distance between the two level lines is the amount the hip rafters will need to be lowered.

tor like the Construction Master® from Calculated Industries®, Inc. However, I prefer to get my figures from a book of rafter tables, such as *Full Length Rafter Framer* by A. F. Riechers.

First, I find the page in the book that lists the rafter lengths for a 4-in-12 pitch roof. The length of a common rafter for a span of 18 ft. 6 in. is listed as 9 ft. 9 in. The length of the hip rafter for the same span is 13 ft. 5¼ in. These distances are from the plumb cut at the center of the ridge to the plumb heel cut of the bird's mouth at the outside of the wall. If the calculation method is based on run instead of span, don't forget to split the span figure in half.

Because these lengths are figured to the center of the ridge, the actual rafter length has to be shortened by half the thickness of the ridge (drawing, p. 34). For a 2x ridge,

common rafters must be shortened ¾ in., and because hip rafters meet the ridge at a 45° angle, they have to be shortened 1¹⁄₁₆ in. These amounts are subtracted from the rafter by measuring out at 90° to the ridge plumb cut.

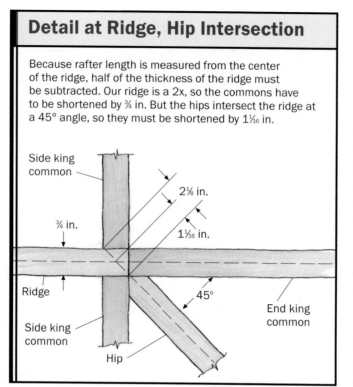

Detail at Ridge, Hip Intersection

Because rafter length is measured from the center of the ridge, half of the thickness of the ridge must be subtracted. Our ridge is a 2x, so the commons have to be shortened by ¾ in. But the hips intersect the ridge at a 45° angle, so they must be shortened by 1¹⁄₁₆ in.

Side king common

2⅛ in.

¾ in.

1¹⁄₁₆ in.

Ridge

45°

Side king common

End king common

Hip

Because pairs of jacks land on opposite sides of the hip, the 45° plumb cuts have to be laid out on opposite sides of each pair of rafters.

Lay Out Rafters in Stacks of Similar Lengths

Once all of the rafter lengths have been determined, it's time to lay out my stock for cutting. I usually use the house plans to get a count of the rafters, keeping in mind that a hip roof has an extra common rafter on each end. Using a pair of low site-built horses, I rack up all of the commons on edge with the crowns up. Next, I flush the ridge ends by holding the face of a 2x4 against the end of the rafters and pulling the rafters up to it one at a time with my hammer claw. From the flushed end, I measure down my length on the two outside rafters, shortening my rafter measurement for the ridge. I snap a chalkline across the tops of the rafters as a registration mark for aligning the bird's mouth on the rafter template.

I then place my common-rafter template against the first rafter flush with the ridge end and scribe the ridge plumb-cut line. I slide this rafter to one side and continue down the line, leaving all of the rafters on

edge. Next, I align the bird's mouth registration mark on the template with the chalkline on the rafters and mark my bird's mouth cutlines on each rafter. When all of the rafters are marked, I cut the ridges, moving the rafters over one at a time. Next, I flip the rafters onto their sides and cut the bird's mouths, overcutting my lines just enough to remove the wedge without weakening the tail section (photo, below). I leave the rafter tails long and cut them to length after all of the rafters are in place.

A Double Cut Brings the End of the Hip Rafter to a Point

I try to pick out long, straight stock for the hips. The hip rafters need to be long enough to include the overhanging tail, which is longer than the tails on the commons. Most carpenters like to give hip rafters a double-side (or bevel) cut at the ridge so that they will fit nicely into the corner formed by the end and side king commons (drawing, above). I do this by laying the hip-rafter template on the rafter stock and marking the ridge cut (left drawing, p. 33). I then slide the pattern down 1½ in. and make a second mark parallel to the first. With my saw set at 45°, I cut along the first line in

Bird's mouths are overcut. A wedge shape is cut out of each rafter to give it a place to land on the plate. These bird's mouths can be overcut just enough to remove the wedge.

one direction and the second in the opposite direction, which leaves me a pointed end that will fit in between the king common rafters.

I set the hip stock on edge and flush up the pointed ridge ends (photo, right). Then I measure down from these points and make my plumb-heel-cut reference marks, shortening the rafters 1 1/16 in. for the 2x ridge. Now the registration mark on my hip template can be aligned with the marks on my rafters, and I can scribe the bird's mouths.

To scribe the hip-rafter tails to the proper width, I hold a pencil against the tail part of the hip template and slide the template along the length of the tail. The bird's mouth of the hip rafters is cut just like the common rafters, and the tails are ripped to complete the cutting.

Jack Rafters Are Cut in Pairs

Jack rafters run parallel to the king commons and frame in the triangular roof sections between the king commons and the hip rafters. They are nailed in pairs into both sides of the hip rafter with each pair cut successively shorter as they come down the hip. The difference in length between each pair of jack rafters is constant (it's called the common difference), and it can be found in the rafter tables. For jack rafters spaced at 16 in. o. c. at a 4-in-12 pitch, the difference in length is 1 ft. 4 7/8 in. For 24-in. spacing, the difference is 2 ft. 1 1/4 in.

I lay out the jacks by racking together eight pieces of rafter stock the same width but slightly shorter than the common rafter (photo, right). (I rack eight pieces because there is a pair of jacks of equal length for each of the four hips.) Next to these I rack eight more pieces a foot or so shorter than the first eight and so on for each set of jack rafters. When the jack-rafter stock is laid out, I flush up the tail ends this time. The tails of the jack rafters are the same length as the tails of the commons, so I snap a line

All four hip rafters are laid out and cut at the same time. Short site-built sawhorses hold the rafter stock for layout and cutting. With all of the boards stacked together, only one set of measurements needs to be taken. Templates (photos, p. 31) do the rest.

Jack rafters are laid out four pairs at a time. Jacks oppose each other in pairs along both sides of the hip rafter. Each successive pair is shorter by a specified length than the pair above it. Diagonal marks remind the author to make his 45° cuts in opposite directions.

The hips and king commons come together at the ridge. The end of the ridge is the meeting point for all of the major framing members of the hip roof. After the end king common is nailed in, the hip rafters are installed, and the ends of the side king commons are nailed in next to the hips.

If the roof is long, additional ridge sections may be installed using other pairs of common rafters for support.

at that distance across all of the edges for my plumb heel cuts.

Next I lay an unshortened common rafter alongside my rack, lining up its heel-cut line with the heel-cut line on the jack stock. From the ridge cut of this common, I measure down the common difference. I shorten this first set of eight jacks by 1⁄16 in. just like the hip rafter and make diagonal marks in opposite directions on each pair of jacks to remind me which way my cuts will go (bottom photo, p. 35). For each successive set of jacks, I measure down the common difference in length from the previous set. These measurements do not need to be shortened by the width of the hip rafter because I subtracted 1⁄16 in. from my first measurement.

Using the common-rafter template, I mark the plumb side cut and the bird's mouth cut. Because pairs of jacks land on

opposite sides of the hip, the 45° plumb cuts have to be laid out on opposite sides of each pair of rafters.

Assemble Common Rafters First

If everything is cut accurately, the roof members should fit together like a puzzle. I always tack down plywood sheets on top of the ceiling joists for a safe place to work. The ridge length and rafter layout can be taken directly from layout on the wall plate, but I prefer to bring up a ridge section and begin my rafter layout about 6 in. from one end. I like having this extra length to compensate for any discrepancies in my layout.

With a partner, I set up my first pair of side king commons and nail them to the plate and into the ceiling joist. (In high-wind areas, rafters may need to be tied to the plates with metal framing anchors.) Next, I go to the other end of the ridge and nail in another set of commons.

The ridge board then gets pulled up between the two sets of commons and nailed in place. I just tack the side king commons to the ridge until the end common has been installed. At this point I make sure the ridge is level by measuring from the tops of the ceiling joists at each end. I support the end of the ridge with a 2x4 leg down to a ceiling joist or to an interior wall and run a diagonal sway brace to keep everything in place temporarily. Next, I slide one of my side king commons out of the way, hold the end king common next to the ridge and mark the end of the ridge. After the ridge is cut to length, I nail my end king common in place.

Next, a hip rafter is toenailed to the wall plate directly over the outside corner. The side cut on the ridge end gets nailed to the end common next to the ridge. I nail the opposing hip in place, and the two-side king commons can be slid back against the hips and nailed in permanently.

If the roof is long, additional ridge sections may be installed using other pairs of common rafters for support. Again, I make sure additional ridge sections are level. At the other end of the building, I mark and cut the ridge and assemble the hips and side king commons as at the first end.

Frieze Blocks Stabilize the Rafters

Before nailing in the jack rafters, I sight down the hip rafter and make sure it is straight from the ridge to the plate. If it's bowed, I brace it straight temporarily until the jacks are in. I start with the longest pair of jacks and nail them to the plate along with frieze blocks, which are nailed in between the rafters at the plate (photo, p. 29).

Local codes don't always call for frieze blocks, but I use them to stabilize rafters and provide perimeter nailing for roof sheathing. If necessary, they can be drilled and screened for ventilation and are a good way to use scrap lumber. I cut a bunch of blocks ahead of time to either 14½ in. or 22½ in., depending on my rafter spacing.

Frieze blocks can be installed flush with the wall, where they serve as backing for the exterior siding. However, with this method the blocks need to be ripped to fit below the roofline. Another method is installing the blocks perpendicular to the rafter just outside the plate line. I like this second method because it requires no ripping and provides a stop for the top of siding.

I nail in the frieze blocks as I install the remaining pairs of jack rafters. Each jack is nailed securely to the hip rafter; I take care not to create a bow. Once all of the pairs of jacks are installed, the hip will be permanently held in place.

The corner frieze blocks get an angled side cut to fit tight against the hips. Once all of the jacks and commons are nailed in, the rafter tails can be measured, marked, and trimmed to length. Remember to measure the overhang out from the wall and not down along the rafter. For this building the overhang is 20 in., and the fascia stock is 2x (1½ in. thick). I mark a point on the top edge of the rafters 18½ in. straight out from the walls at both ends of the building and snap a line across the rafters between my marks. I extend my chalklines out over the tails of the hip rafters to mark the overhang at the corners. When marking the plumb cut on the rafter tails, use the common-rafter template on the commons and the hip template on the hips.

Larry Haun *has been building houses for over 50 years. He is the author of several carpentry books including,* Habitat for Humanity How to Build a House, *published by The Taunton Press. His website is www.carpentryforeveryone.com.*

Sources

A. F. Riechers
Box 405
Palo Alto, CA 94302

Calculated Industries Inc.
4840 Hytech Dr.
Carson City, NV 89706
800-854-8075

Ceiling Joists for a Hip Roof

■ BY LARRY HAUN

If you want a simple roof, go for a gable. The angles are basic, and even the ceiling framing is a snap because it generally runs parallel to the rafters. A hip, however, is a roof to reckon with, and not just because of its angles. With rafters sloping up from all four sides of the building, how do you joist the ceiling?

"No problem," you say. But what about the joists that run perpendicular to the rafters on opposing sides of the house? Depending on the roof's slope, it's quite likely that you won't have much room for the joist closest to the plate: the rafters will be in the way. In 41 years of pounding nails, I've seen several solutions to the problem of joisting a hip roof.

Time-Honored Solutions

Depending on the size of the joists, the ones closest to the plates may need to end at a header to let the hip rafter through (photo, facing page). A similar header is sometimes required for the valley rafter. Backing for the ceiling finish is obtained by nailing 2x blocking flatwise to the plates between the rafters (behind the frieze blocking), to pro-

vide 1½ in. of nailing surface for the ceiling drywall.

There are times, however, when the first joist may have to be held away from the plate as much as 32 in., depending on the pitch of the roof and the size of the lumber used for the joists. The traditional method of filling the space between the outside wall and this first joist is to add stub joists at right angles to the main joists, parallel to the jack rafters (photo, p. 41). This technique often requires that the first joist be doubled to carry the extra ceiling load. The stub joists are usually clipped on one end to keep them from sticking up above the roof framing; pressure blocks at the other end help to support them.

A Better Solution

There's another way to handle the problem, one that requires less material and labor. Set your last joist as close as possible to the plate. Then set another one—flatwise— within 16 in. of the outside wall. There will be plenty of room between it and the underside of the hips and jacks. The next step is to install the rafters and to nail frieze and backing blocks between them as described earlier. Then cut strongbacks from scrap 2x

Heading Out the Joists

Hip rafter

Header

Blocking

Plate

stock and run them flatwise from the plate to the first on-edge joist (photo, p. 40). You won't need many of them; spacing them about 4 ft. o. c. should do.

Secure the strongbacks to the backing blocks and to the upright joist with a couple of 16d's at each end. At the joist end the strongbacks must be held up 1½ in. from the

Strongback Framing

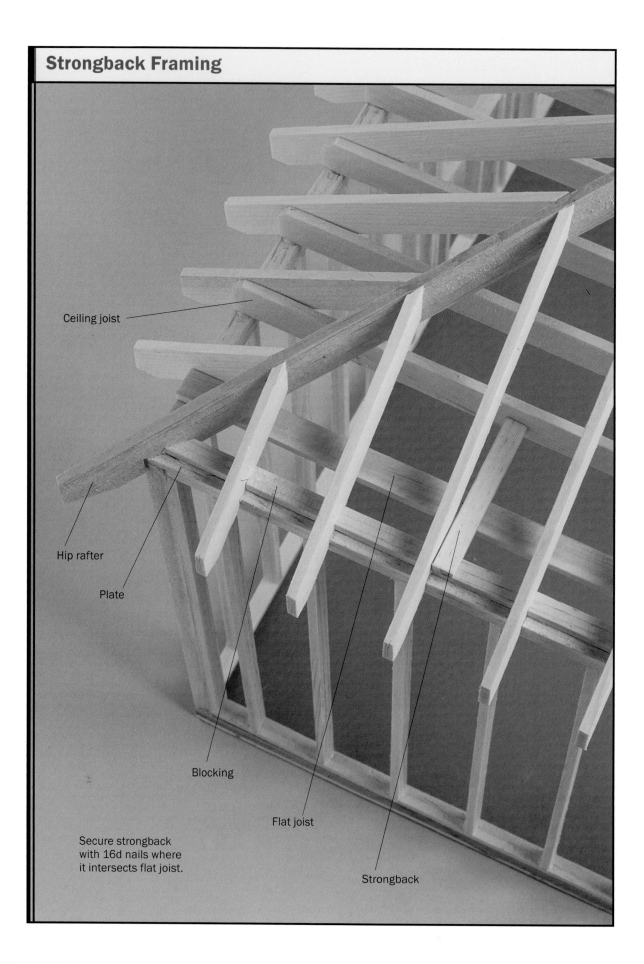

Ceiling joist

Hip rafter

Plate

Blocking

Flat joist

Secure strongback
with 16d nails where
it intersects flat joist.

Strongback

Stub-Joist Framing

Pressure blocks

Ceiling joist

Stub joists

Plate

The end corner of each stub joist must be cut flush with the plane of the roof.

bottom. Finally, pull the flat joist up to the strongback, securing it with three or four more 16d's, angling them slightly for better holding power. The strongbacks will stiffen and support the flatwise joist. With this step complete, the ceiling is ready and you're set to move on.

Larry Haun *has been building houses for more than 50 years. He is the author of several carpentry books including,* Habitat for Humanity How to Build a House, *published by The Taunton Press. His website is www.carpentryforeveryone.com.*

Framing a Dutch Roof

■ **BY LARRY HAUN**

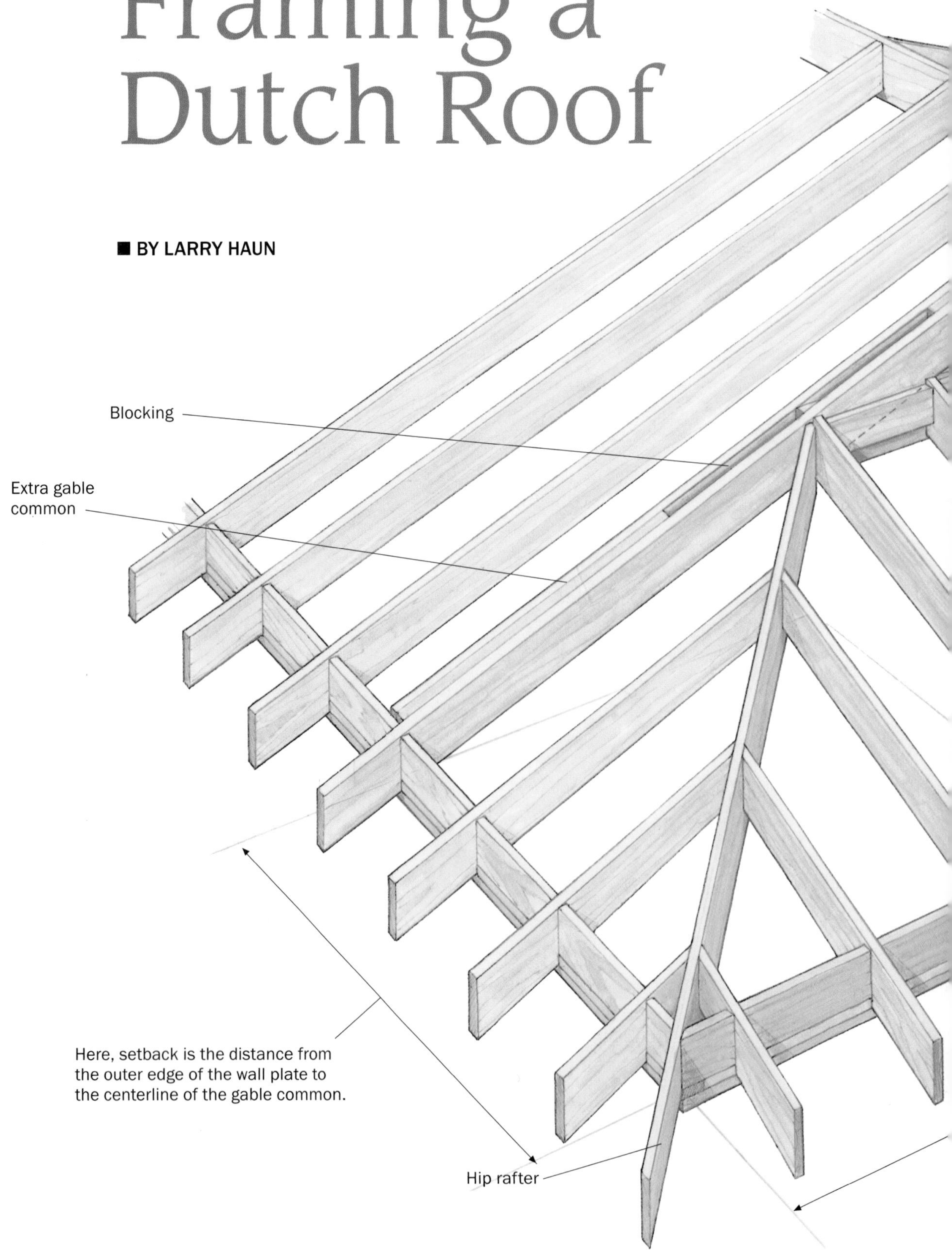

Blocking

Extra gable common

Here, setback is the distance from the outer edge of the wall plate to the centerline of the gable common.

Hip rafter

Components of a Dutch Roof

A dutch roof combines a gable roof and a hip roof. The gable is framed first, with the first set of gable-common rafters placed a set distance from the end of the building. The hip roof is fastened to the first gable rafters, which are reinforced to support both the hip rafters and the Dutch ridge.

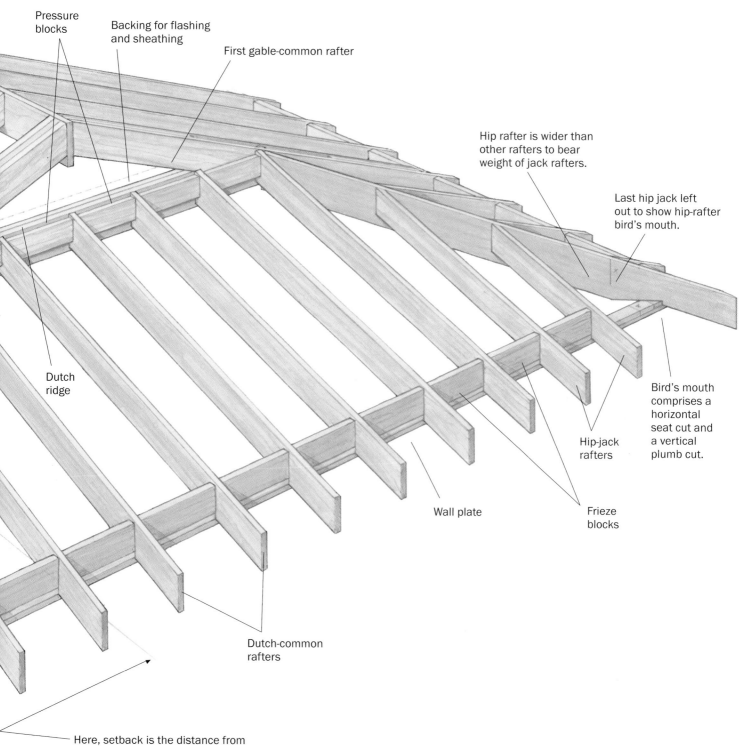

Pressure blocks

Backing for flashing and sheathing

First gable-common rafter

Hip rafter is wider than other rafters to bear weight of jack rafters.

Last hip jack left out to show hip-rafter bird's mouth.

Dutch ridge

Hip-jack rafters

Wall plate

Frieze blocks

Bird's mouth comprises a horizontal seat cut and a vertical plumb cut.

Dutch-common rafters

Here, setback is the distance from the outer edge of the wall plate to the centerline of the Dutch common.

I recall the first time I was given house plans with a Dutch roof (sometimes called a Dutch hip or Dutch gable). The plans looked difficult even though I already knew how to frame both a gable and a hip roof. When I realized that the Dutch was really just a combination of the roofs I already knew how to frame, the plans looked simple, and the roof went together fairly easily. Since then, I've framed plenty of Dutch roofs.

Build the Gable First

The Dutch is a section of hip roof in which hip rafters run into a gable end instead of going up to a ridge (drawing, pp 42–43). Exactly where the gable interrupts the hip is called the setback, the distance from the end of the building to the first set of gable-common rafters. When stick framing a Dutch roof, I begin by checking the plans for the amount of setback. A long setback means that the roof will show more hip than gable; a short setback shows more gable than hip.

On the house we featured here, the plans specified a 5-in-12 slope on the gable roof with setback of 5 ft. 6 in. to the center of the first pair of gable-common rafters. I lay out this distance on the top plates and cut and build the gable section of the roof.

Use Rafter Tables to Lay Out Commons, Hips and Jacks at the Same Time

The hip section of the Dutch roof requires several framing members: hip rafters that run 45° from the corners, Dutch-common rafters that run perpendicular to the gable end, and hip-jack rafters that die into the hip rafters. To figure out the lengths of all of these framing members, I use the setback distance, 5 ft. 6 in., and the roof pitch, 5-in-12, and I consult a rafter table such as *The Full Length Roof Framer*, available from

A. F. Riechers. You also could use a ft./in. calculator.

The 5-ft. 6-in. setback is also the run—the horizontal distance covered by the rafter as seen in the plan view—of the Dutch-common rafters. Doubling this figure gives me the span, the dimension necessary for using most rafter tables. In this case the span is 11 ft., and the rafter table's common-rafter column shows the length of the Dutch-common rafters for this roof as 5 ft. 11½ in. to the center of the Dutch ridge. I subtract half the ridge thickness, ¾ in., to find the exact plate-to-ridge length of the Dutch-common rafters; then I mark and cut them.

Jack rafters are laid out in pairs and cut with a bird's mouth on one end just like the commons, but they have a 45° cheek cut (photo, below) where they butt into the hip rafter. The first pair of jacks is shorter than the common rafter, and each successive pair

Here, the author uses a different template to scribe a cheek cut on a jack rafter.

is shorter than the previous pair. The difference in length is the common difference and can be determined using the rafter table. For a 5-in-12 pitch, the common difference for jacks spaced 16-in. o. c. is 1 ft. 5⅜ in.

Scribing and Cutting Hip Rafters

The lengths of hip rafters are listed under the hip/valley column in the rafter table. For a 5-in-12 pitch, the hip for an 11-ft. span is 8 ft. 1¼ in. This is measured from the ridge (a Dutch ridge in this case) to the plumb cut at the end of the bird's mouth.

Just like common rafters, hips have to be shortened by half the thickness of the ridge. Unlike commons, which meet the ridge at a right angle, hips come in at 45°, so they have to be shortened by half the 45° thickness of the ridge, or 1⅟₁₆ in. This dimension yields an adjusted hip-rafter length of 8 ft. ⁵⁄₁₆ in.

A Dutch roof has two hips, so I place two pieces of hip stock, crowns up, on the horses. Hip stock should be 2 in. wider than the commons and long enough to include the tail that forms the overhang. The plans call for an 18-in. overhang; the actual length of the hip tail, about 26 in., comes from the rafter table.

I mark the ridge plumb-cut location square across the top edges of the hip stock, then scribe the plumb lines with a hip-rafter template. (A rafter template is like a short rafter in that it's got the ridge cut, the bird's mouth, and the rafter tail all on a piece of 1x the same width as the rafter but only about 2-ft. long. I make templates for each type of rafter in a roof.) The ridge plumb cut can be a 45° cheek cut or a double-side cut: two 45° plumb cuts that form a point. I've never been convinced that one cut is better than the other, but on this roof I made a double-side cut just for the sheer enjoyment. To make this cut, I use the tongue of the framing square to mark a second plumb-cut line 1 ½ in. away from the first one. With the saw set at 45°, I make the first side cut; then I go on to make the second cut in the opposite direction.

Next, I flush up the ridge ends of the hip stock, measure out 8 ft. ⁵⁄₁₆ in. (the adjusted rafter length) and mark for the heel plumb cut on the top edge of the rafters. I align the hip template's registration mark with the mark for the heel cut on the hip stock and scribe the bird's mouth, which, because this is a hip rafter, has a deeper seat cut than a common rafter (photo, above). Then I use the template to scribe the tail part of the hip rafter and rip it down to the width of the common and jack rafters.

The Dutch Ridge Is Scribed in Place

The next step is to use a Dutch-common rafter to mark the location of the Dutch ridge that hangs between the first pair of gable commons. I place the Dutch common flush alongside each gable common, seat cut

Rafter templates speed layout. Position a hip-rafter template to mark the bird's mouth. Hips are wider than commons and jacks, so the left half of the template is used to scribe the hip tail, which must be ripped down to the width of the jacks and the commons.

Use the Dutch commons to locate the Dutch ridge. Using a Dutch-common rafter as a template, mark its plumb cut on the first gable common. After the opposing gable common is marked, the Dutch ridge will sit even with the top of these lines.

The Dutch ridge is nailed between the first pair of gable-common rafters. After striking a chalkline to position the top of the Dutch ridge, nail the 2x10 ridge between and under the 2x8 gable commons. The Dutch-common rafters hang from this Dutch ridge.

to seat cut, and scribe the plumb cut (top photo, facing page).

Next, I pick out a 2x that's 2 in. wider than the Dutch commons. This 2x will be the Dutch ridge, which supports the top ends of the Dutch commons. With a little help, I hold the ridge stock in place against the gable commons so that it crosses them at the top of the plumb lines I've just scribed. I scribe each end of the ridge by marking on the underside of the gable common; then I cut the ridge to length. Next, I spike the ridge in place up under the commons with several 16d nails (bottom photo, facing page). Later, I'll reinforce it with a backer.

Blocking Separates and Strengthens the Rafters

Now, I pull up the hip rafters, position them directly over the outside corners and fasten them to the wall plate with two 16d toenails on one side and one on the other. I nail off rafters at the plate first with the hip rafter centered on the corner. At the ridge, the plumb cut lies flat against the gable commons. I drive three 16ds through the commons into the hips.

The 5-ft. 6-in. setback means that the first set of Dutch commons is positioned 5-ft. 6-in. o. c. from the corners of the building. Each common is nailed to the top plate with two 16d toenails on one side and one 16d on the other. At the ridge, the first Dutch commons butt against the side cuts of the hip rafters, and they're spiked in place with two 16ds.

Next, I nail with three 16ds a 14½-in. pressure block, a 2x block the same size as the common, to the Dutch ridge and tight against the common (photo, above). The front edge of the pressure block is flush with the common. The pressure block helps keep the rafter in place.

At the plate line a 14½-in. 2x frieze block is nailed between each rafter with one 16d

Blocking prevents twisted rafters. The author nails a 2x pressure block to the Dutch ridge. A pressure block goes between all of the Dutch commons.

at one end and two at the opposite end. This block helps keep the rafter from rolling over and strengthens the roof structure. Then I install another common and another pair of blocks and so on until I get to the jack rafters.

Before nailing in the hip-jack rafters, I sight down the hip rafter and make sure it's straight from the ridge to the plate. If the hip is bowed, I temporarily brace it straight until the jacks are nailed in place. Then, beginning with the longest jack, I nail it at the plate against a 14½-in. frieze block, driving two 16ds into the block and one 16d toenail into the plate on each side of the jack. I nail each jack to the hip with three 16d nails, taking care not to bow the hip rafter from side to side. Once the opposing jack is nailed in, the hip is locked in place. Then I install the rest of the jacks and frieze blocks.

Once all the jacks and commons are nailed in, the overhangs can be measured, marked, and trimmed to length, and the fascia can be nailed on. The length of the hip

Once all the jacks and commons are nailed in, the overhangs can be measured, marked, and trimmed to length, and the fascia can be nailed on.

Sources

A. F. Riechers
Box 405
Palo Alto, CA 94302
(800) 250-5189
www.afriechers@aol.com

**Calculated
Industries, Inc.**
4840 Hytech Dr.
Carson City, NV 89706
800-854-8075
www.calculated.com

**2x6 backing strengthens the Dutch ridge. Be-
cause the Dutch ridge only was nailed under the
gable commons, a backing ridge is face nailed
to the gable commons and to the Dutch ridge
for added support.**

**Double the first gable for support. The gable
end supports the hip roof, so a second set of
gable commons is installed. The gap is filled
with 2x blocking.**

overhang is determined simply by extending
the chalkline on the commons all the way
across the hip. When cutting rafter tails to
length, I check to be sure I'm using the
common-rafter template on the commons
and the hip-rafter template on the hips.

The Dutch Ridge
Needs Extra Support

With all the rafters in place, it's time to reinforce the ridge and commons holding the
upper part of the Dutch roof. I nail a long
2x, 2 in. wider than the Dutch ridge, to both
the Dutch ridge and the two supporting
gable commons (left photo, above). The
ends of this backing ridge are flush with the
top of the gable commons.

Next, I place another set of gable commons against the backing ridge, space them
from the two ridge-supporting gable commons with 2x blocking, and nail the new set
of gable commons to the plate, the gable
ridge and the backing ridge (right photo,
above). This second set of gable commons
and the backing ridge provide plenty of
support for the Dutch roof. The last step is
to hold a 2x6 directly over the Dutch ridge,
mark, cut, and nail it to the backing ridge.
This 2x6 acts as backing for flashing needed
between roofing materials and siding.

*Larry Haun has been building houses for over
50 years. He is the author of several carpentry
books uncluding,* Habitat for Humanity How to Build
a House, *published by The Taunton Press. His website is www.carpentryforeveryone.com*

Joining Unequally Pitched Roofs

■ BY GEORGE NASH

The intersection of two roofs with unequal pitches involves geometrical relationships not readily visualized or easily understood. Graphic projections can be intimidating to anyone without substantial framing experience. As for me, I want to frame the roof, not tinker with models, pens, paper, and a calculator. In fact, I'm convinced that "fear of ciphering" is so common that few framers have anything more than a vague notion of somehow using "strings and levels" to lay out complex roofs. This sometimes translates into blundering through, trial-by-error or fudge-and-fix techniques, with hopes that the client doesn't show up until the roof sheathing has hidden the mistakes.

That's how it went for me until a summer when everything I built had a weird roof. I needed a framing method that was fast, accurate, relatively simple, and, most of all, nonmathematical. I've forgotten all the trigonometry I never learned in high school, so I'm hopelessly doomed to be a string-and-level man. In the article that follows, I'll describe that method for you and apply it

to a house I built that's fairly typical of unequally pitched roof framing.

Purists, or those more mathematically adept than I, may find my methods inelegant, or perhaps less precise than the computational approaches. I'll tell you this, though: the tolerances are well within the width of a pencil line, the mechanics are easily understood, and the method works for me.

First Things First

In the project drawings I was given, the L-shape of the Stoecklein house appeared to include a conventional valley, but it didn't. According to the drawings, the ridge was at the same height for both roofs, but the rafter span of the main roof was 22 ft. while the ell span was only 16 ft. The main roof was framed at a 7-in-12 pitch. In order for a smaller span to terminate at the same eaves height, the pitch of the ell had to be steeper.

The first rule for framing uncommon rafters is to lay out and install all the rafters that ain't (in other words, do the common

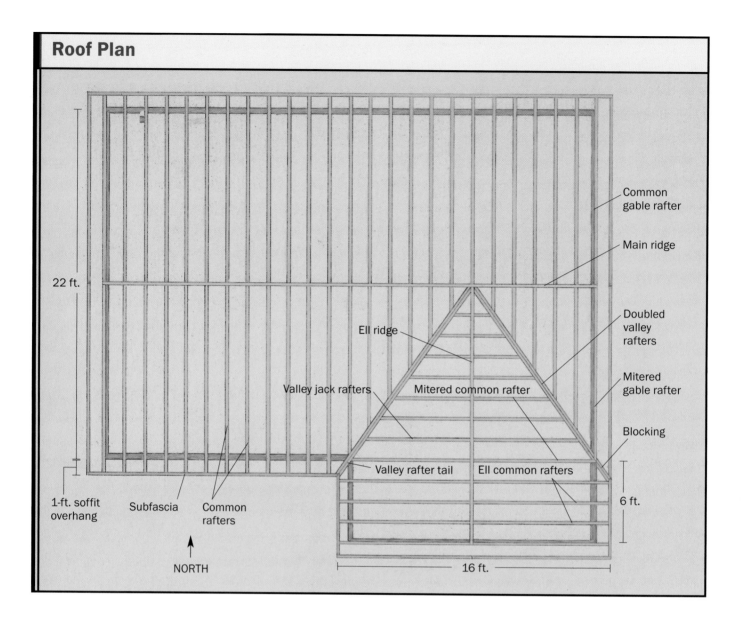

Common gable rafter

Main ridge

Doubled valley rafters

Mitered gable rafter

Blocking

6 ft.

Ell ridge

Valley jack rafters

Mitered common rafter

Valley rafter tail

Ell common rafters

22 ft.

1-ft. soffit overhang

Subfascia

Common rafters

NORTH

16 ft.

rafters first). After cutting and installing all the rafters on the main roof, I was ready to tackle the ell.

Installing the Ridge

As for framing the roof of the ell, the idea is to work from the top down, which means getting the ridge into place and then installing the rafters. The first step was to measure and mark the midpoint of the ell top plate and center a plumbed and braced 2x4 post over it. This would support the outboard end of the ell ridge until the ell's common rafters were installed. The post was cut to the same length as the distance between

the top plate and the underside of the main ridge. Working from pipe scaffolding, I transferred the centerline of the ell onto the main ridge to locate the intersection of the ell ridge. (I always use rented pipe scaffolding for roof framing. With two sections and enough staging plank, all but the longest roofs can be framed with minimal movement.)

Figuring the length of the ell ridge was easy. It had to run the full length of the ell, plus half of the full width of the main building, minus one-half the thickness of the main roof's ridgeboard. In this case, that meant 6 ft. (the ell) plus 11 ft. (half the main roof) minus ¾ in. (half the ridge).

So the ell ridge would be 16 ft. 11¼ in. long. After cutting the ell ridge to length and marking out the rafter spacing on it (better now than when it's up in the air), I nailed it into place at the main ridge and atop the ell centerpost. I double-checked to make sure that the end of the ell ridge ended plumb over the gable wall. A temporary diagonal brace run down to the deck held everything in place.

Ell Common Rafters

Once the ridges and main-roof common rafters were in place, the layout for the ell common rafters was simple: I pinned rafter stock against the end of the ridge board and the corner of the wall plate and scribed for the plumb cut and bird's mouth (drawing, top right). No, it's not elegant, but it works perfectly. The position and depth of the bird's mouth followed from the rule that the seat cut should begin at the inside edge of the top plate. The length of the rafter tail will determine how far away from the wall the fascia will be, so the rafter tails on the ell had to be laid out to allow the ell fascia to flow continuously into the main fascia. Rather than including this step in the initial layout, I simply made the plumb cut at the ridge and the bird's-mouth cuts, leaving ample tail stock to be trimmed later. I cut two rafters and tacked them to the ridge to test the fit.

With the two test rafters in place, it was easy to lay out the cuts on their tails. First I leveled across from the bottom edge of a main-roof common rafter tail to the wall it-self, as if laying out a horizontal soffit look-out, and then measured the distance from this mark to the top of the wall plate. Re-turning to the ell, I measured down the wall this same amount and snapped a level line across the wall. Then it was short work with a level and a pencil to extend this line across the bottom of the extending rafter tails; this would be the level cut (drawing, bottom right). To get the plumb cut, I moved a

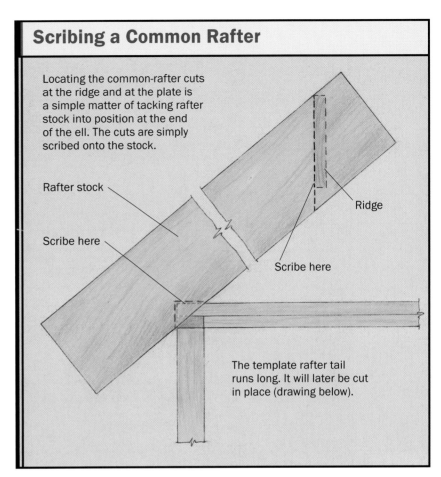

Scribing a Common Rafter

Locating the common-rafter cuts at the ridge and at the plate is a simple matter of tacking rafter stock into position at the end of the ell. The cuts are simply scribed onto the stock.

Rafter stock

Scribe here

Ridge

Scribe here

The template rafter tail runs long. It will later be cut in place (drawing below).

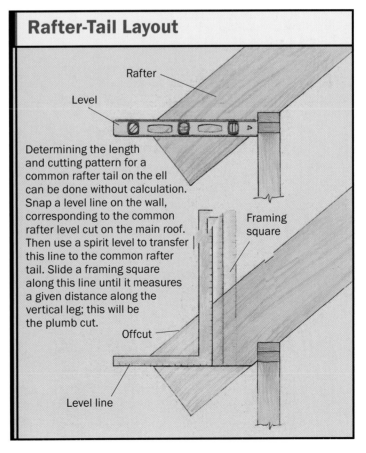

Rafter-Tail Layout

Rafter

Level

Determining the length and cutting pattern for a common rafter tail on the ell can be done without calculation. Snap a level line on the wall, corresponding to the common rafter level cut on the main roof. Then use a spirit level to transfer this line to the common rafter tail. Slide a framing square along this line until it measures a given distance along the vertical leg; this will be the plumb cut.

Framing square

Offcut

Level line

framing square horizontally across this line until it measured a vertical line equal in length to the plumb cut of the main-roof rafters.

It's important to note that if you want the intersecting ridges to be of the same height and the fascias on both parts of the house to line up, the width of the ell soffit will be less than that of the main soffit. If the ell were wider than the main roof, the reverse would be true. If you'd rather have the soffits be equal in width and at the same elevation all around the house, then one of the ridges must be lowered or raised accordingly. Usually these sorts of details are worked out in the design phase. On this job, the difference in soffit width amounted to slightly less than 3 in., which really isn't noticeable.

Although the method I just described will establish the tail cut for either horizontal or

pitch soffits, I'd recommend using a horizontal soffit unless the design is beyond your control or changes are not allowed. Horizontal soffit boards and vents are much easier to fit and nail than pitched ones.

About this time I'll usually support the intersecting ridges with a temporary post. Otherwise the ridges could sag as the valleys and their jack rafters are added, and the plumb cuts and lengths of the jack rafters would become increasingly inaccurate. I always check the ridges for straightness, or line them to a string, before laying out the valley rafters.

Finding the Valley Length

A valley rafter has a lot of cuts and angles to line up, and you'll have a lot of lumber to throw away if one calculation turns out

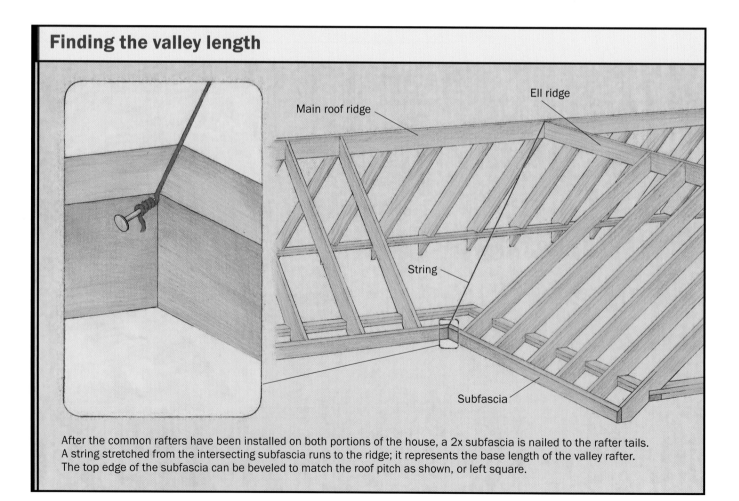

Finding the valley length

After the common rafters have been installed on both portions of the house, a 2x subfascia is nailed to the rafter tails. A string stretched from the intersecting subfascia runs to the ridge; it represents the base length of the valley rafter. The top edge of the subfascia can be beveled to match the roof pitch as shown, or left square.

wrong. Fortunately, there's a way to isolate each component and reduce the chances for confusion and error.

Because I always use a subfascia of 2x stock (for the extra support it gives to the soffit), finding the length of the valley rafter isn't tough. First, I nailed the subfascia to all the common rafters around the house. Where the ell intersected the main building, I extended the subfascias to meet at the inside corner (drawings, facing page). Because I had beveled their top edges to match the corresponding roof pitches, it took some fudging with a trim plane to fit the steeper bevel to the shallower one. Some carpenters skip the bevel and simply drop the fascia slightly instead (either method will provide a nailing surface for the edge of the roof sheathing). Then I nailed the intersecting subfascias together. I stretched a string from the outside corner of this intersection to the intersection of the two ridges, right to the top edge; this represented the center line of the valley rafter's top edge. Finding the actual rafter length was simple: I just measured along the string.

Figuring the Plumb Cuts

To find the face angle and the edge angle of the valley-rafter plumb cuts, I used a sliding T-bevel to copy the angle between the string and the ridges. The same angle marked the heel cut of the bird's mouth. It was easy to use a short level and plumb up from the wall plate to the string and then measure the distance to determine not only the heel cut, but the depth to the seat cut of the bird's mouth and the length of the valley from ridge to plate (drawings, right). The tail cut was simply the same angle repeated where the string crossed the intersecting subfascia. Before making the actual cuts I transferred the angles to a short length of stock and cut a test piece—mistakes on scrap stock are a lot easier to correct.

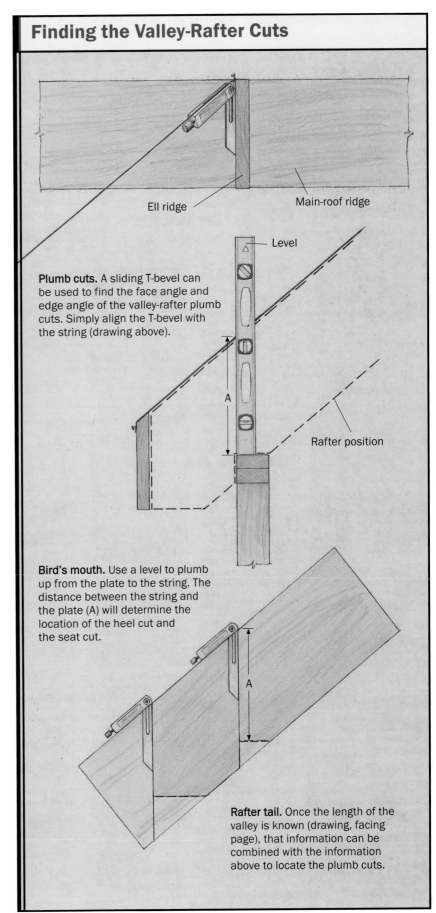

Finding the Valley-Rafter Cuts

Ell ridge

Main-roof ridge

Level

Plumb cuts. A sliding T-bevel can be used to find the face angle and edge angle of the valley-rafter plumb cuts. Simply align the T-bevel with the string (drawing above).

A

Rafter position

Bird's mouth. Use a level to plumb up from the plate to the string. The distance between the string and the plate (A) will determine the location of the heel cut and the seat cut.

A

Rafter tail. Once the length of the valley is known (drawing, facing page), that information can be combined with the information above to locate the plumb cuts.

A Doubled Valley

A valley rafter on a roof with regular pitches calls for a double cheek cut where the valley rafter intersects the ridges and the subfascia.

A valley rafter on a roof with regular pitches calls for a double cheek cut where the valley rafter intersects the ridges and the subfascia. The top edge of the valley rafter then has to be "dropped" just enough to allow roof sheathing to clear it. But the double cheek cut can be complicated, and dropping the valley leaves very little support for fastening the roof sheathing. That goes against the grain of my framing aesthetic—I like plenty of meat to nail into. That's why I double the valley rafter. And if the top edge of each doubled valley rafter is beveled to match the plane of the adjacent roof, the rafter will provide a much better nailing surface for the sheathing (drawing, below).

Of course, two trial pieces with single cheek cuts already made are needed, one for each half of the doubled valley. To find the angle of the top bevels, I lined up each of my trial pieces with the valley rafter center-line string and held it at the intersection of the two ridges. Then I scribed it where the stock projected above the ridge. This is called backing the valley. Because the resulting angle will be scribed across the face of the compound angle (the ridge plumb cut) and not the square edge of the rafter stock itself, it can't very easily be duplicated with a T-bevel. Instead, I used trial and error—when the cut of the table saw matches the scribe line, I've got the right angle. After the top bevels were cut, I installed the paired rafters and spiked them together.

By the way, the same benefits of doubling the valley rafter apply when it must support a finished ceiling. In that case, a 2x4 ripped to the required width and bevel will furr out the underside of the double rafter for solid nailing, and the finished intersection of the different ceiling planes will be more accurate.

While I left a tail on the doubled south-west valley rafters, letting them intersect the fascia, I dispensed with tails on the south-east valley rafters where the ell shared a common wall with the main-roof gable. Instead, I cut a 45° miter in the plate end of the main roof's gable rafter and did the same thing with the intersecting common rafter of the ell. This way they'd fit against each other at the outside of the wall plate and automatically give the correct height for the center-line string. In lieu of the valley rafter tail, the soffit was fastened to a lookout and blocking above carried the edge of the roof deck.

By the way, I left the center-line strings in place until all the valley jack rafters were finished. Even a doubled valley rafter will shift with the push and shove of the jack rafters and the weight of the carpenters as they clamber about, especially if the span is long. The string is a convenient guide for

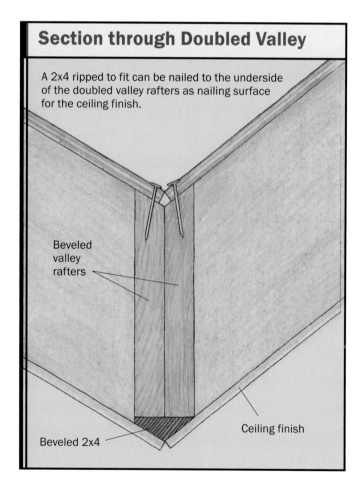

Section through Doubled Valley

A 2x4 ripped to fit can be nailed to the underside of the doubled valley rafters as nailing surface for the ceiling finish.

Beveled valley rafters

Beveled 2x4

Ceiling finish

Making Cheek Cuts

The worst thing about jack rafters is making the cheek cut, which is almost always greater than 45°. Sawing through a 2x12 at a compound angle with a handsaw is tedious and tiresome; using a chainsaw is dangerous and usually not very accurate, and I don't have a compound miter saw. Instead, I used applied geometry, some power, and a dash of old-fashioned elbow grease.

For example, suppose the edge angle figures out to be 72° and the face angle 35° (drawing, below). I first cut the face angle across the face of the rafter (with the saw set at 90°) and then tack the rafter to the sawhorse. Complementary angles must add up to 90°, so the complement of 72° is 18°. If I set the saw at an angle and then hold its base against the edge cut itself (perpendicular to the side of the rafter) I can make a 72° cut. Although a 7¼-in. blade will not cut all the way through the angle, what's left is fairly easy to finish with a handsaw. An 8¼-in. or 12-in. circular saw would be handier. I know of no easier way to make these cuts than on a radial-arm saw, which takes more time to set up.

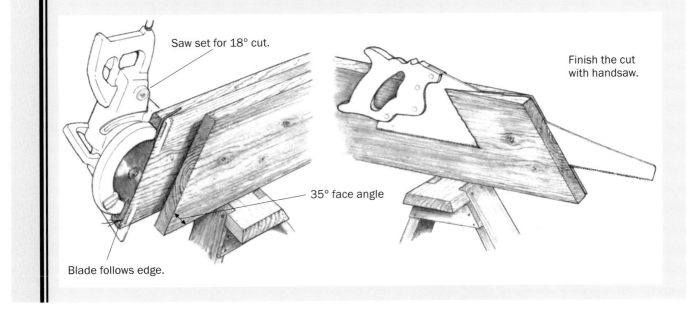

Saw set for 18° cut.

Finish the cut with handsaw.

35° face angle

Blade follows edge.

constantly checking alignment. Temporary braces may be needed to hold the valley rafter to the line until all the framing is complete.

The Valley Jack Rafters

I have found that the tables of common differences for jack and hip rafters on lines 3 and 4 of the framing square don't always lead to perfect cuts. There are just too many 16ths and smidgens in a real framing job for it to correspond exactly with a theoretical frame. And because I was dealing with an odd pitch on this project, I wanted to derive the common difference (the uniform difference in length between each successive jack) by measuring the actual distance between the first two jack rafters, not by consulting a table. It was string and level time, phase II.

The layout lines for the jack rafters were already marked on both ridges. All I had to do was make a corresponding tick mark on the valley rafter at the right place to find the length and face angle of the jack. I knew that the center of the jack would have to be 16 in. away from the center of the nearest common rafter and be parallel to it, so I was

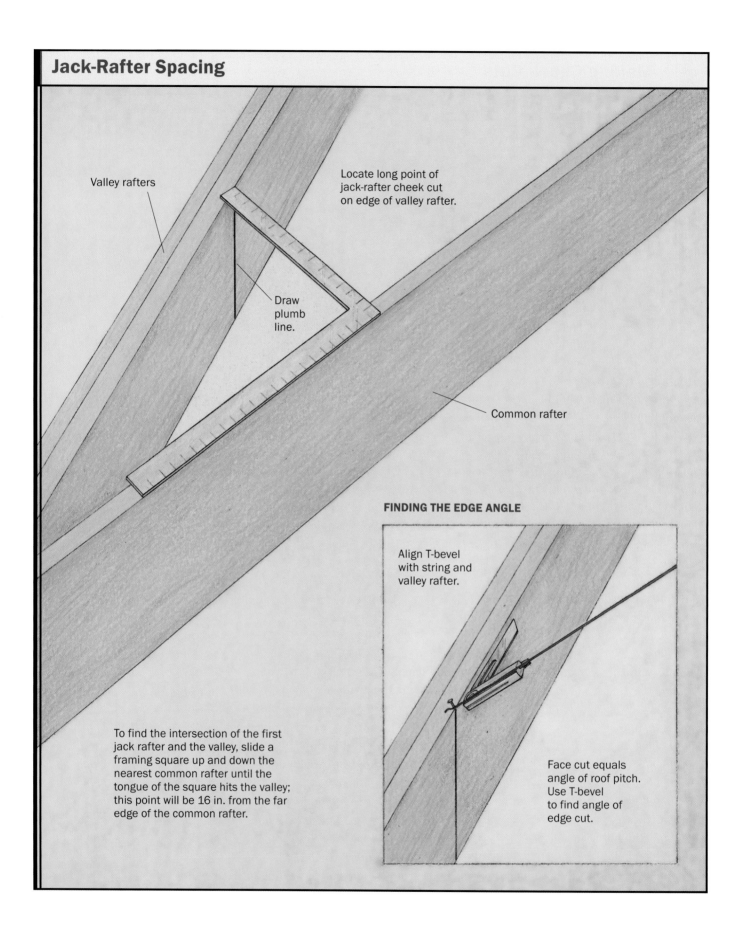

Valley rafters

Locate long point of jack-rafter cheek cut on edge of valley rafter.

Draw plumb line.

Common rafter

FINDING THE EDGE ANGLE

Align T-bevel with string and valley rafter.

To find the intersection of the first jack rafter and the valley, slide a framing square up and down the nearest common rafter until the tongue of the square hits the valley; this point will be 16 in. from the far edge of the common rafter.

Face cut equals angle of roof pitch. Use T-bevel to find angle of edge cut.

able to use my square to pinpoint its intersection with the valley. (You'll have to eyeball the common rafter for straightness and take out any bows by bracing with a temporary board before you try this.) With the long side of the square resting on top of the common rafter and the short side resting on the valley rafter, I simply slid the square up and down until I located a point on the outside of the valley exactly 16 in. away from the outside of the common rafter (drawings, facing page). This represented the intersection of the valley jack with the valley. Then I drew a plumb line down the side of the valley rafter using a short level.

I fastened a string from the top of this mark to the ridge, parallel to the common rafter, and stretched it tightly. Then I aligned the body of the T-bevel with the string and set the blade against the valley rafter; this gave me the angle of the cheek cut. It's important that the blade and the center of the T-bevel handle be in the same plane when lined up to the string; a small twist will give you an incorrect angle. Here again, you'll want to make a trial piece from scrap stock to test the fit before cutting the actual rafter. Because the valley had been doubled up earlier, instead of dropped, the point marked was exact.

To determine the jack-rafter length I simply measured the string from the ridge to the tick mark on the valley rafter. I duplicated the angle of the plumb cut at the ridge on each successive piece using a framing protractor. Making the compound cuts first before laying out the plumb cut at the ridge end ensures a good fit. The string was no longer needed once I found the angles and verified the fit.

After I installed the first jack rafter, it was easy enough to determine the common difference simply by measuring it. All I had to do now was repeat the series of cuts on each remaining jack rafter, reducing the length of each one by the common difference.

To keep the valley rafter in line, the jack rafters are usually nailed home in opposing pairs. But with unequal roof pitches, the cheek cuts are not mirror images and the spacing intervals will not line up across from each other. To avoid throwing subsequent measurements off, I find it easier to work up one side of the next jack rafter by setting the framing square along the edges of the last. I used bracing to keep the jacks from crowding the valley rafter off the center line.

The beauty of this empirical method is that no advance preparation is required before framing can begin. A good rule of thumb is: if you count the jack rafters for one side of the valley as if they were common rafters and add an extra, there won't be much waste. The shorter jacks are usually cut from the leftovers of the longer ones.

George Nash lives in Burlington, Vermont, and winters in Safford, Arizona.

TIP

To avoid throwing subsequent measurements off, work up one side of the next jack rafter by setting the framing square along the edges of the last.

Simplified Valley Framing

■ BY LARRY HAUN

The foreman on one of my first framing jobs asked me if I knew how to build a California roof. I had to admit I didn't. Instead of firing me on the spot, the foreman gave me until the next morning to learn. I pored over my carpentry books at home that night, and I found what I was looking for under "blind valley." That after-hours discovery nearly 40 years ago helped me keep my job, and the framing technique I learned is just as useful to me today.

When framing two gable roofs that meet at right angles, and when one of the roofs has a lower ridge than the other, the common approach is to use a supporting valley rafter that extends from the wall plate to the main roof ridge, and a shorter nonsupporting valley rafter that intersects it. But jack rafters must then be cut to fill the triangular space between the ridge and the valleys on the main roof (left drawing, facing page). And a second set of jack rafters is needed for the smaller roof. All of that takes time.

The blind valley, or California roof as it's called out here, often is a less-complicated way of handling the same situation (right drawing, facing page). The technique certainly makes sense when framing an addition because the new roof can be framed directly on the old roof. It also works well in new construction when the room under the main roof has a cathedral ceiling. Although this is most often used when a smaller roof intersects a main roof, the same technique can be used when the ridge heights of the two intersecting roofs are the same.

I was stumped by this framing problem as a green carpenter back in the 1950s, but the technique is not difficult. The main roof is framed, and the roof sheathing is applied. Then the common rafters of the smaller, intersecting roof are erected, and the ridge is carried over to the main roof. Finally, the valley jack rafters of the smaller roof are cut and installed, linking the ridge of the smaller roof with the deck of the main roof. The photos in this article show this technique

No valley rafters. When framing two roofs that intersect, the common method is to use valley rafters (left drawing, facing page). A faster method (right drawing, facing page) is to sheath the main roof first, then frame the smaller roof on top of it.

Two Methods for Framing Valleys

CONVENTIONAL METHOD

Common rafter

Jack rafter

Ridge

Valley rafter

SIMPLIFIED METHOD

Common rafter

Ridge

Jack rafter

Main roof sheathing

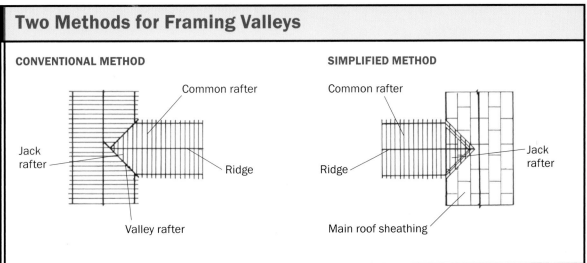

Mark the ridge length. To find the correct length for the ridge extension, measure from the end of the existing ridge to the point you have marked on the main roof deck. Or lay the ridge extension on top of the existing ridge, run the extension all the way to the main roof and then mark the extension where it should be cut (right).

Scribing the ridge. To mark the correct angle on the ridge extension where it meets the main roof, you can use a scrap of wood and the main roof deck. Set the extension on top of the secondary ridge already in place, make sure it is level and then use a 2x scrap to scribe the angle on the extension (below).

being used to frame a new roof on an existing roof covered with a membrane.

Some building codes require full sheathing under the secondary roof to maintain the main roof's shear strength. Full sheathing is certainly what you would use when building an addition onto an existing roof. At minimum, the main roof must have sheathing where the secondary roof ridge and jack rafters land. You may need to leave a hole in the sheathing on the main roof to allow passage for people or ductwork.

Extending the Ridge

Once the main roof has been built and the sheathing applied, the common rafters of the secondary roof are raised. The inboard end of the ridge extends to the main roof if the stock is long enough. If not, the ridge needs to be extended. To find where the ridge should meet the main roof, sight along the length of the ridge and mark the point

where the top of the ridge falls on the main roof. A measurement from the mark on the main roof deck to where the secondary ridge ends gives you the length of the ridge extension (top photo, facing page).

You can use your framing square to mark the angle on the end of the ridge extension that will make the ridge snug on the main roof. The angle will be the same as for the seat cut on the common rafters. But I usually scribe the angle in place (bottom photo, facing page). I set one end of the ridge-extension stock on top of the secondary ridge, and the other end on the main roof at the point where the ridge will end up—the ridge extension should be sitting level at this point. Then I use a scrap of 2x ridge stock to scribe the angle of the main roof onto the ridge extension. Once the ridge extension has been

measured and cut, nail it in place on top of the main roof sheathing, making sure it is level and straight. At the other end, toenail the extension to the end of the ridge already in place (photo, above).

Marking Valley Locations

Now you can mark the location of the valleys on the main roof sheathing. You will need to snap a chalkline from the end of the extended ridge where it meets the main roof to a point near the eaves where the two roof planes come together (top photo, p. 62). To find the lower mark for the valley chalkline, extend the plane of the secondary roof into the main roof—with a stringline or a piece of 2x stock—and find a spot where the two

Nailing it up. Once the ridge extension has the correct angle on one end and has been cut to length, toenail it to the end of the ridge already in place and to the existing roof deck.

intersect. Snap the chalkline from the ridge, through the spot that you've marked.

You must add support along this line as a base for the tail ends of the valley jack rafters—the short rafters that extend from the valley to the ridge of the secondary roof. Make this base by nailing two 1x6s side by side, or by using strips of plywood 12 in. to 16 in. wide, next to the valley chalkline. Don't nail them on the line. Instead, hold the boards back from the line so that the top edge of the jack rafters will be in the same plane as the line (photo, below). The steeper the pitch, the closer to the line the boards will be. To find the exact distance between the chalkline and the 1x6, stretch a line from the ridge of the secondary roof to the chalkline in the valley and push your 1x6 up to the string.

This support material can just be marked in place on the roof and cut roughly to length. Total accuracy isn't required. Nail the support boards in place with 8d nails through the sheathing and into the common rafters of the main roof.

Snapping the line. After the ridge extension is in place, snap a chalkline to mark the location of the valley. The upper point is where the ridge extension meets the main roof. The lower point is found by extending the plane of the secondary roof into the main roof. In this example the wall of the addition is higher than the wall it intersects on the existing structure.

Installing support material. The doubled 1x6 supports in the valley are set back from the chalkline. The steeper the roof, the smaller the distance between the support and the line.

Jack Rafter Cuts

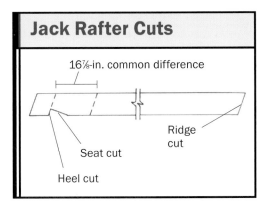

16⅞-in. common difference

Ridge
cut

Seat cut

Heel cut

Cutting the Jack Rafters

The ridge extension can now be filled in with jack rafters. They are laid out in pairs, one jack for each side of the ridge. The first pair of jacks will be shorter than the common rafters, and each successive pair will be shorter as they move along the secondary ridge and up the main roof. The amount that each jack is shortened depends on both the pitch of the main roof and the on-center spacing of the rafters. But each succeeding jack rafter on a roof will be shortened by the same amount, called the common difference. There are several ways to determine this common difference. An easy way is to use a book of rafter tables. Turn to the chart showing the pitch for the main roof (in our example 4-in-12) and find the on-center spacing for the rafters (in this case 16 in. o. c.). Or you can use the table stamped on the blade of your roofing square. The common difference for a 4-in-12 roof is 16⅞ in. So as you move up the valley cutting the jacks, each pair would be 16⅞ in. shorter than the pair before.

To mark the first pair of jack rafters, use a duplicate of a common rafter from the secondary roof and lay it on edge next to two pieces of rafter stock that are approximately 1 ft. shorter. Then add two more pieces of rafter stock about a foot shorter than the first pair. Keep adding successively shorter pairs of rafter stock until they shrink to nothing and keep the ends flush at the ridge

Marking the jack rafters. The valley jack rafters are marked in pairs, one for each side of the ridge. The angled marks indicate the direction of the bevel (side cut) on the level seat cut. Set your saw to the correct bevel and make sure the blade is angled in the same direction as the slash mark on the edge of the stock.

end. Measure up from the heel cut of the common rafter exactly 16⅞ in. and scribe a mark on the edge of the longest pair. Measure 16⅞ in. from that mark and lay out the next pair and so on until all are laid out.

Each pair of jack rafters will have a plumb cut at the ridge (just like the common rafter) and a level seat cut with a bevel (side cut) on the opposite end to fit the pitch of the main roof. The side cut at the lower end tips either to the right or to the left, depending on which side of the ridge the jack is to be nailed. To indicate this for cutting purposes, make angled slash marks, one to the right and one to the left, on each pair of jacks (photo, above). These marks will help you lay out and cut the correct side cut later.

So far, I have assumed that the last common rafter on the secondary roof falls exactly in the corner. In that case the first jack rafter would be a full 16⅞ in. shorter. If the last common does not fall exactly in the corner, the difference would not be as great, and you'll have to measure to find the length of the first jack. Lay out 16 in. along the ridge and the valley from the last common rafter. Measure from the ridge to the point on the valley chalkline to get the length of the first pair of jack rafters. After that, each pair will be 16⅞ in. shorter than the previous pair.

Making a Template

To mark the seat and the ridge cuts on the jack rafters, make a pattern or template (photo, below). On one end of a short piece of 1x material that's about the same width as the rafter stock, scribe a ridge cut by holding the tongue of the framing square on 4 in. and the blade on 12 in., and mark along the tongue. The level seat cut is drawn on the other end of the scrap by marking along the blade. After cutting along these two lines, nail a 1x2 fence on the top edge to make it easy to keep the template even with the top edge of the stock.

Now, with the template, mark the ridge cuts on all the jack rafters. For the seat cuts, place the template on the jack stock so that the point of the seat cut lines up with the intersection of the length and slash marks you made earlier—this is the long point on the bottom of the jack rafter. Each jack rafter of a pair will get a line for the seat cut—but on opposite sides.

When you're ready to make the seat cuts at the ends of the rafters, your rafter tables will also provide the correct bevel for the side cut. Set your saw to this angle (for a 4-in-12 roof, the bevel is 18½°) and cut along the lines you made with the template. As you cut, make sure the sawblade is angled in

A template will help. To mark rafters accurately, make a template from a piece of 1x material that's the same width as the rafter. Make a ridge cut on one end and a level seat cut on the other. A 1x2 nailed on the top edge of the template acts as a fence to aid alignment.

Installing the jack rafters. Once the valley jack rafters have been measured and cut, they are installed along the ridge just as if they were commons. Toenail them into the 1x6 supports.

When eaves heights are unequal. When the intersecting walls are at different heights, a scrap piece of rafter stock or plywood nailed to the backside of the last common on the smaller roof will prevent birds from nesting in the eaves and will simplify the shingling process.

the same direction as the slash mark you made on the edge of each jack rafter.

This sounds more difficult than it really is, and it will be obvious when you start doing it. One jack is cut to the left, one to the right. When you're done, you will have pairs of jack rafters that are cut to the same length, but the bevels of the seat cuts will be in opposite directions.

Once the jack rafters are cut, lay out the ridge at the correct spacing (in this example 16 in. o. c.) and nail the jack rafters into place. Use two 16d nails, just like you would for a common rafter. Nail the seat cut to the 1x6 base. Secure these jacks to the base by toenailing them through the sides so that no nails will be in the way if you have to cut sheathing.

Finishing Touches

If two intersecting roofs have different eaves heights—as is the case on the addition I framed for this article—you may need to fit a scrap of plywood or rafter material behind the common rafter where the two roofs meet. On a roof with open eaves (i.e., no soffit), this prevents birds from nesting in this corner, and it doesn't leave an unreachable section of roof for the shingler.

If the roofs intersect at the same plate height, you will need to cut a fake valley rafter tail out in the overhang, so the sheathing for both roofs is supported where it intersects.

Larry Haun has been building houses for over 50 years. He is the author of several carpentry books including, Habitat for Humanity How to Build a House, *published by The Taunton Press. His website is www.carpentryforeveryone.com.*

Framing a Bay Window with Irregular Hips

■ BY DON DUNKLEY

My crew and I frame houses in central California, near Sacramento, where designers compete with one another to see who can create the most complicated roofs. To stay in business, the local carpenters have to be adept at framing every type of roof— hip, gable, octagon, cone—sometimes all in the same building.

One modest and enduring feature that turns up in many of these homes is the bay window popout. The kind we build most frequently, and the subject of this article, consists of two 45° corners and a projection, or offset, of 2 ft. (floor plan, p. 70). It is 10 ft. wide at the wall line and 6 ft. wide at the front of the offset. The plate height of the bay and of the adjoining room are 8 ft. 1 in., and the roof pitch is 8-in-12.

A hip roof commonly tops this kind of a bay. But unlike many of the hip-roof bays that get built locally, we frame ours

with two irregular hips (bottom photo, facing page). More often than not I run across roof plans that leave out a second irregular hip. Without it, the plane of the roof has to be warped to intersect the valley (top photo, facing page). Once you become aware of this refinement, chances are you'll spot many an example of incorrectly framed bays on a casual drive down a residential street. Adding the second irregular hip allows the roof planes to meet at crisp angles.

Building a roof with one pair of irregular hips is a challenge—add another pair and it's a task for a journeyman carpenter. When I first started out as a framing carpenter, I spent a lot of time laying out the rafter locations on the subfloor, then transferred them by way of plumb bobs and stringlines to temporary staging, where another session with stringlines and tape measures would

Leaving the second irregular hip out of a bay-window roof causes an awkward warp in the sheathing, which shows up in the shingling and the valley flashing (top photo, facing page). The bay in the bottom photo was framed with both hips, and the valley runs straight and true.

Building a roof with one pair of irregular hips is a challenge—add another pair and it's a task for a journeyman carpenter.

Opposing walls are joined by a tie beam across the top of the opening to the bay. The upper half of the top plate has been let into the beam for several feet.

diagonal, I enter 11 ft. as rise, 14 ft. as run, punch the diagonal button, and the calculator will read 17 ft. 9⅝ in. When I punch the convert-to-feet-and-inches button, it tells me 17 ft. 9⅝ in.

The second tool is a book called *Roof Framing*, by Marshall Gross (Craftsman Book Company). Gross uses a technique to lay out roofs that he calls the "height above plate" method (HAP). Simply stated, the HAP system allows me to set the ridges first at their actual height. Then I bring the rafters to meet them. I've found this system to be unbeatable for assembling complex roofs. But before we dive into HAP and bay window/roof theory and calcs, let's look at layout and walls.

Patterns and Plates

We build bays like the one shown in the photograph at left on either slab or wood-framed floors, and sometimes on cantilevered joists. In each case, laying out the bay begins after the subfloor is in place and I've snapped a chalkline marking the inside edge of the wall plates around the house.

To save time and ensure accuracy when I mark the position of the bay, I use a plywood pattern of a 2-ft. by 2-ft., 45° corner (floor plan, p. 70). By placing the pattern long the wall line at the beginning of the bay, I can quickly lay out a perfect 45° wall. The pattern has layout marks on both sides, so I can flip it to lay out the opposite corner.

I usually make square cuts on the ends of the diagonal wall plates. They abut outer wall plates that have two 45° cuts on their ends (floor plan, p. 70). I do this for two reasons: The angled stud on the outer wall plate gives me a good nailing surface to anchor the walls together, and it gives me a little more room to squeeze the window into the diagonal wall. Designers inevitably want lots of windows in these walls. That means I need from 26½ in. to 27½ in. for my header, depending on the width of the windows. As you can see from the photo on the facing

follow as I puzzled out seat cuts and cheek cuts. No more. I've incorporated two tools into my roof-cutting procedures that do away with all the plodding.

The first is a Construction Master Calculator from Calculated Industries, Inc. This calculator works in feet and inches and also metric. It also has pitch, rise, run, diagonal, regular and irregular hip/valley functions, which eliminate some of the key strokes required to apply standard calculators to carpentry work. For instance, instead of using a square-root formula to find a

The author nails down irregular hip rafter A on a cantilevered bay. Note the 1x4 king studs in the diagonal walls. They allow more room for the window.

page, this can get snug. To make the windows fit, I sometimes have to use 1x4 king studs instead of 2x4s next to the trimmers that carry the window headers.

After the walls have been framed and plumbed, it's time for the roof. If you're familiar with roof theory, I'll go straight to calculating the rafters for the bay. If you'd like to brush up on roof basics, refer to the sidebar, "Regular and Irregular Hips," on pp. 74–75.

Locating the Ridge

To find the ridge height using the HAP method, I add the distance the rafter sits above the plate at the seat cut to the theo-retical rise, minus the reduction caused by the thickness of the ridge (elevation view, p. 72). For example, our seat cut (the horizontal portion of a bird's mouth) is 3½ in. on the level, giving a 4¼-in. rise above the plate for a 2x6 rafter. The run of the common rafter is 5 ft., and the rise is 40 in. (8-in. pitch by 5-ft. run). This gives us a theoretical rise of 44¼ in. If there were no ridge, the peak of the rafters would be this height, but the ridge comes between them and must be accounted for. This applies to both common rafters intersecting the ridge at a right angle or, as in this case, a common rafter in line with the ridge. I find the reduction the "new-fashioned" way, courtesy of

If I later cut all my rafters accurately, and my walls have been properly plumbed, lined, and braced, all the parts will converge to lock the assembly together.

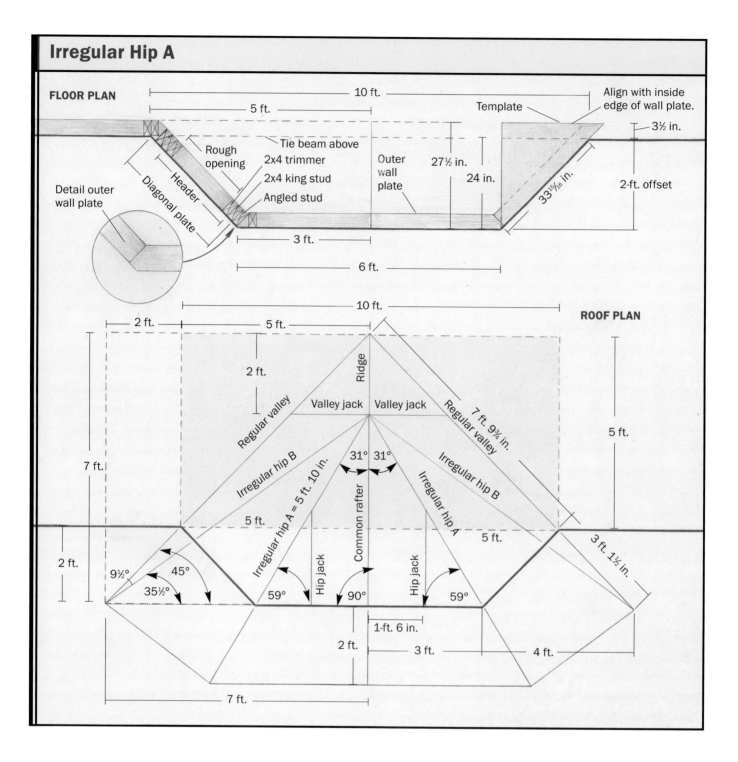

FLOOR PLAN

10 ft.

5 ft.

Template

Align with inside edge of wall plate.

3½ in.

Rough opening

Tie beam above

2x4 trimmer

2x4 king stud

Angled stud

Outer wall plate

27½ in.

24 in.

33¹⁵⁄₁₆ in.

2-ft. offset

Detail outer wall plate

Header

Diagonal plate

3 ft.

6 ft.

ROOF PLAN

10 ft.

2 ft.

5 ft.

Ridge

7 ft. 9¾ in.

5 ft.

2 ft.

Regular valley

Valley jack

Valley jack

Regular valley

7 ft.

Irregular hip B

31° 31°

Irregular hip B

Irregular hip A = 5 ft. 10 in.

Common rafter

Irregular hip A

5 ft.

5 ft.

3 ft. 1½ in.

2 ft.

9½°

45°

35½°

Hip jack

Hip jack

59°

59°

90°

1-ft. 6 in.

2 ft.

3 ft.

4 ft.

7 ft.

Construction Master (detail 1, p. 72). Our ridge is 1½ in. thick. Using my Dimensional Calculator, I enter half the thickness of the ridge (¾ in.) as the run. Next I enter 8 in. as the pitch, and punch the rise button. My answer is ½ in. I subtract that from 44¼ in. to get the actual height of the ridge above the plate: 43¾ in.

To begin erecting the bay's roof, I set its ridge on temporary legs so that it sits precisely 43¾ in. above the plate. If I later cut all my rafters accurately, and my walls have been properly plumbed, lined, and braced, all the parts will converge to lock the assembly together.

Because the offset of the bay is 2 ft., the ridge is approximately 2 ft. long. Actually, it's a little longer in order to compensate for the shortening allowance of the common rafter. More on this in a minute.

First, the Valleys

Our floor plans show a 2-ft. offset and a 6-ft.-long front of the bay window. The interior opening of the bay is 10 ft. wide. The roof plan shows two valley rafters, one common rafter, and two sets of irregular hip rafters (roof plan, p. 70). The roof overhang is 2 ft.

At this stage of the roof framing I'm not concerned about the 45° wall of the bay. Instead, I'm thinking about the 10-ft.-wide opening to the bay. Dividing it in half gives me a pair of 5-ft. squares in plan. The bay's ridge and common rafter form a line between the squares, and its regular valleys are the diagonals.

An 8-in-17 valley (see the sidebar on pp. 74–75) on a 5-ft. run calculates to be 7 ft. 9¾ in. long. To get my 2-ft. overhang, I have to add 3 ft. 1½ in. from the seat cut to the tail cut. The vertical edge (heel cut or plumb cut) of the bird's mouth aligns with the exterior face of the wall framing.

The skinny little lines we see when we look at roof framing plans represent the center lines of rafters and beams. To transfer the ideal of a line with no width into a rafter that is typically 1½ in. thick, we have to take the shortening allowance (SA) into consideration. For a regular hip or valley, the SA is equal to half the thickness of the common rafter, cut on a 45° angle (detail 2, p. 72). That works out to 1¹⁄₁₆ in. for 2x framing lumber. Remember this is a level measurement, and has to be adjusted for the pitch of the roof. For our 8-in-17 pitch, the valley rafter has to be shortened by 1³⁄₁₆ in. To find the adjusted SA with the Construction Master, enter the pitch as 8 in., then enter the thickness of the common (¾ in.) as run and punch the hip/valley key to get the adjusted SA of 1³⁄₁₆ in.

I'm in the habit of cutting double cheek cuts on valley rafters. Often there are other

Converging rafters meet at the end of the bay's ridge beam. In the lower left corner of the photo you can see where the valleys intersect the ridge. The "X" marks one end of the 2-ft. ridge.

rafters intersecting the same ridge, and the double cheek cut gives me a little extra room for adjustment. In addition, to save time at the cutting table I put double cheek plumb cuts on all my valley and hip stock at the same time, and then decide later which ones end up as hips or valleys. The photo above shows how the valleys intersect the ridge.

Common Rafter

In order for the common rafter to be at the same height as the valley rafter, it also must be calculated on the 10-ft. span, or 5-ft. run. An 8-in-12 common on a 5-ft. run calculates to be 6 ft. ⅛ in. long. Measured on the level, its SA is half the thickness of the ridge—in this case ¾ in. (detail 1, p. 72).

Our next move is to calculate the lengths of the valley jacks. Since our run from the common rafter to the valley rafter is 2 ft., our valley jack will be cut on that run. The

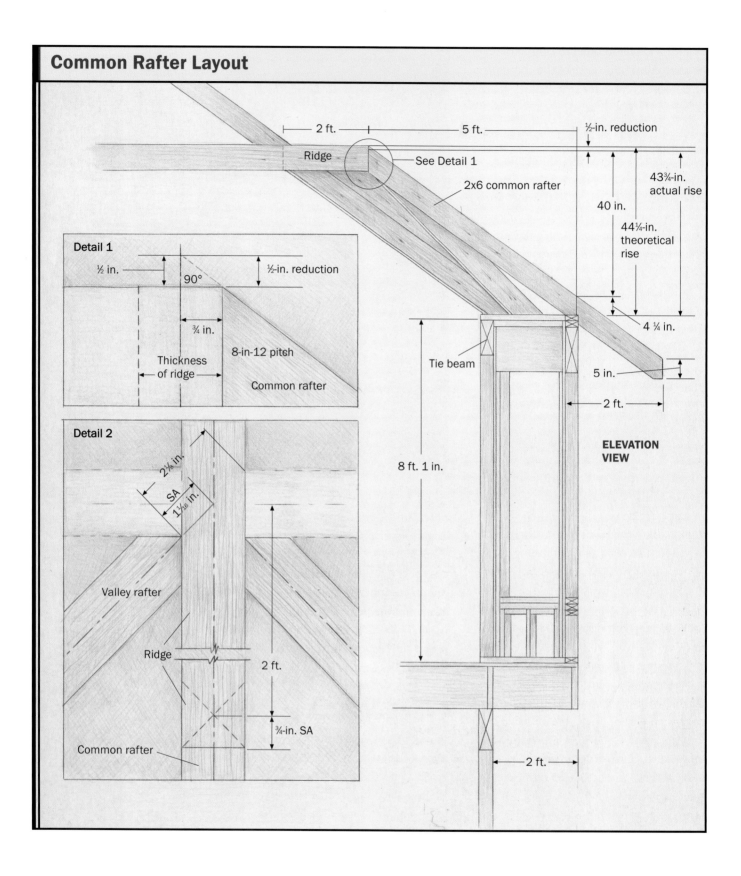

Detail 1

½ in.

90°

½-in. reduction

¾ in.

Thickness of ridge

8-in-12 pitch

Common rafter

Detail 2

2⅜ in.

SA

1⅟₁₆ in.

Valley rafter

Ridge

2 ft.

¾-in. SA

Common rafter

2 ft.

5 ft.

½-in. reduction

Ridge

See Detail 1

2x6 common rafter

43¾-in. actual rise

40 in.

44¼-in. theoretical rise

4 ¼ in.

Tie beam

5 in.

2 ft.

ELEVATION VIEW

8 ft. 1 in.

2 ft.

Plan of Rafter Intersection

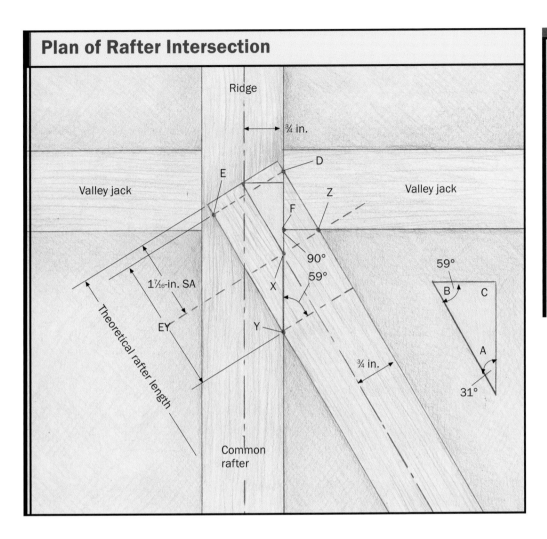

Ridge

¾ in.

D

E

Z

Valley jack

Valley jack

F

90°

59°

1⁷⁄₁₆-in. SA

59°

X

B

C

A

Theoretical rafter length

EY

Y

¾ in.

59°

31°

Common rafter

When you make compound cuts with a circular saw, such as the cheek cuts on a hip or jack rafter, the saw automatically compensates for the pitch of the rafter.

valley jack will have two SAs—one half the thickness of the ridge and one for half the thickness of the valley measured across its top at a 45° angle.

Irregular Hip A

Looking at the roof plan (drawing, p. 70) we see that the distance from the common rafter to irregular hip A is 3 ft. The run of the common rafter to the ridge is 5 ft. To find the run of hip A, I enter 3-ft. rise and 5-ft. run. When I punch the diagonal button, it reads 5 ft. 10 in. But that's measured on the level. To figure the length of hip A, we need its actual rise. By feeding our 40-in. rise and 5-ft. 10-in. run into the calculator, I get the full unadjusted length of the rafter from seat cut to ridge junction: 6 ft. 8⅝ in.

While we're working with these numbers, let's figure out the plumb cut for this hip. After entering the rise and run and getting the diagonal as we did above, simply punch pitch to get our plumb cut of 6⅞ in. The trig tables say that's almost 30°. While the tangent number is still in the calculator's display screen, I punch the convert-to-inches button, which now reads 6⅞ in. That means the pitch (and the plumb cut) of this hip rafter is 6⅞-in-12.

Because we're dealing with an irregular hip here, we need to know the angles formed by its intersection with the plate and the common rafter. Without them we can't calculate the cheek cuts on the hip rafter at the ridge or the cheek cuts on the hip jack rafters. Using the calculator, enter the same 3-ft. rise and 5-ft. run as we did in step 1 of irregular hip A. Now, we will punch the

Regular and Irregular Hips

Understanding complex roofs requires an understanding of the mathematics of a simple roof. Here are some basics.

The pitch of a roof is determined by the relationship of vertical rise to the horizontal run. An 8-in-12 roof means that for every 12 in. of run the rafter will rise 8 in. To represent this relationship visually, a diagonal line connects the two, forming a triangle (detail C). The diagonal represents the slope of the rafter. Because the rise and run are perpendicular to one another, the three lines form a right triangle. The mathematical formula to find the length of the diagonal of a right triangle is called the Pythagorean theorem: $a^2 + b^2 = c^2$. Another way to figure it: c = the square root of $a^2 + b^2$

Fortunately, the carpenter can reach for a calculator to process these numbers. Another way to bypass tedious rafter calculations is with a rafter book, such as *Full Length Roof Framer.* It lists the lengths for common, regular hip and valley rafters for roofs with 48 different pitches.

If you divide the rise by the run, you get the tangent. For an 8-in-12 roof, the tangent is .666667. What can you do with this information? By looking at a table of trigonometric functions you'll find that a tangent of .666667 is equal to approximately 33¾°. Therefore an 8-in-12 roof rises at an angle of 33¾°. All roof pitches have a corresponding tangent/degree.

Once we know two of the angles in a triangle, we can subtract their sum from 180° to get the third angle. In our example, 180° (90° + 33¾°) = 56¼°, which is called the complement of a 33¾° angle (complementary angles add up to 90°). When laid out with a Speed Square, this 56¼° angle will give the level or horizontal cut of a rafter whereas the 33¾° is the plumb cut (detail A).

In plan, a regular hip rafter intersects common rafters at a 45° angle. To understand a hip, look at it from the plan, or top view (left drawing, facing page). The common rafters intersect the plates at

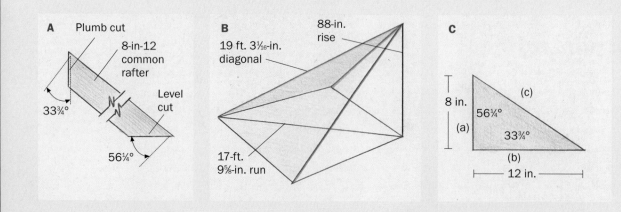

A Plumb cut
8-in-12 common rafter
33¾°
Level cut
56¼°

B 88-in. rise
19 ft. 3¹⁄₁₆-in. diagonal
17-ft. 9⅝-in. run

C
8 in. (a)
(c)
56¼°
33¾°
(b)
12 in.

90°, while the hip is 45° to the plates. In order for the regular hip rafter to reach the same point as a common rafter, its run must be longer. For every 12 in. a common rafter needs for run, a regular hip rafter, regardless of pitch, needs 16.97 in. (for pitch designations, carpenters round the number off to 17 in.). This relationship holds true for regular valley rafters as well. Therefore, a regular hip or valley rafter on an 8-in-12 roof is cut to an 8-in-17 pitch. Divide 8 by 17 to get the tangent: .4705, which gives us the hip plumb cut of 25½°.

As shown in our plan, a regular-hip roof over a 22-ft. span reveals two 11-ft. squares. The run of the commons will be 11 ft. Find the run of the hips by multiplying the run of the common times the run of a regular hip: or, 11 x 16.97 in., which equals 15 ft. 6¹¹⁄₁₆ in.

So what does this tell us about how to calculate irregular hips? To figure out an irregular hip the diagonal length of its run is needed. But because an irregular hip doesn't have a 45° angle in plan, the value of 16.97 can't be used. Back we go to the Pythagorean theorem.

Let's say we have an 8-in-12 roof with commons that run 11 ft., but the commons are 14 ft. from the corner where the hip originates at the plates (right drawing, below). By using the Pythagorean theorem, we find that the diagonal in a triangle with 11 ft. and 14 ft. sides is 17 ft. 9⅝ in., which gives us the run of this irregular hip. To find the full length (also referred to as theoretical or unadjusted length) of the hip rafter, use the rise (88 in.) and the run to find the diagonal, which is 19 ft. 3¹⁄₁₆ in.

The hip jacks are another wrinkle—those intersecting an irregular-hip rafter have different angles on their cheek cuts. Using our tangent formula, we find that our irregular hips divide the plan view of our roof into 38° and 52° angles. When the cheeks of opposing jack rafters are cut at these angles and adjusted for the pitch of the rafter as shown in the bottom drawing on p. 70, they'll fit snug against the irregular hip.

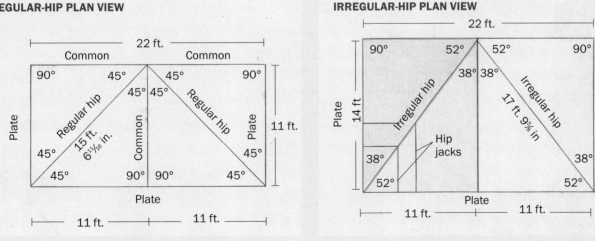

REGULAR-HIP PLAN VIEW

IRREGULAR-HIP PLAN VIEW

Detail 3

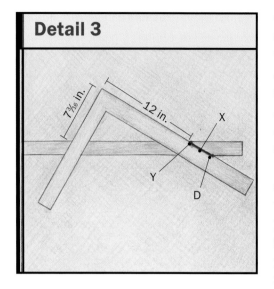

pitch key twice to get the degree equivalent of the pitch, 31°, which is the angle formed at the ridge. The complementary angle to this is 59°, the angle formed on the wall plate. Using the tangent method and the trig tables, I find that the angle made by the hip and the plate is 59; therefore the complementary angle is 31°.

To be an irregular hip is to be off center at the intersection of all the other rafters (plan of rafter intersection, p. 73). Here's a way to calculate the SA and cheek-cut angles for this asymmetrical junction. In the triangle ABC, the rise of BC is half the thickness of the ridge, or ¾ in. The angle A is 31°, derived from the plan view of our roof. Thirty-one degrees is the same as a 7³⁄₁₆-in. roof pitch. Calculator in hand, I enter 7³⁄₁₆ in. as pitch and ¾ in. as rise, punch the diagonal button, and it reads 1⁷⁄₁₆ in. for the hypotenuse AB in triangle ABC. This is the SA, measured on the level. The adjusted SA for this 6⅞- and 12-pitch is 1⅝ in.

Let's take a look at the rafter intersection plan to see how the framing square is used to lay out this irregular-hip plumb cut. First, measure back from the full length of the rafter the adjusted SA, 1⅝ in., to mark point X on the rafter's centerline. By looking at the plan view we see that the hip needs two

different cheek cuts. Let's make the longest side first. By laying the framing square on top of our rafter with the tongue set at 7³⁄₁₆ and the body set at 12, draw a line on the edge of the rafter that passes through point X (detail 3, left). This line (YD) gives us the angle for the cheek cut on the side of the common rafter.

By studying our plan of our rafter intersection, we see that the two cheek cuts intersect off the centerline of the rafter at point F. To find this point, first square a line from the edge of the rafter to X to find point Z. A line perpendicular to YD that intersects point Z gives us the second cheek cut in plan.

Now we've got the cheek-cut angles for a horizontal rafter. Just to make this a challenging exercise, the angles change as the rafter's pitch increases—the greater the pitch the greater the change. You can demonstrate this phenomenon by drawing an equilateral triangle on a slip of paper. Hold the drawing level, with its base toward you. Now slowly rotate the drawing to vertical to change its pitch. You can watch the angle change from an obvious 60° to a right angle and beyond.

Detail 4

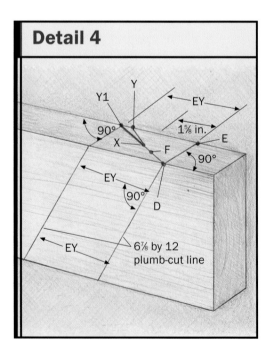

Detail 5

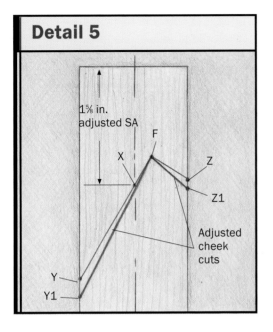

1⅝ in. adjusted SA

F

X

Z

Z1

Adjusted cheek cuts

Y

Y1

Sources

A.F. Reichers
Box 405,
Palo Alto, CA 94302
(800) 250-5189
www.afriechers@aol.com

Calculated Industries, Inc.
4840 Hytech Dr.
Carson City, NV 89706
(800) 854-8075
www.calculated.com

Craftsman Book Company
6058 Corte del Cedro
Carlsbad, CA 92009
(800) 829-8123
www.craftsman-book.com

When you make compound cuts with a circular saw, such as the cheek cuts on a hip or jack rafter, the saw automatically compensates for the pitch of the rafter. But if you have to use a handsaw to cut an angle beyond the circular saw's 45° capability, you have to compensate for the angle change in your layout. The angle we need to cut here is 59°. Here's how to lay it out.

Recall that our hip plumb cut is 6⅞ and 12. Scribe a line at this pitch on the side of the rafter, beginning at point D (detail 4, facing page). Now mark from this line the distance EY on the side of the rafter, and scribe another line at 6⅞ pitch. Square this line across the top of the rafter to find point Y1. Connect point F and point Y1 to find the adjusted cheek cut. If you want to cut the other angle with a handsaw, repeat the process to find the adjusted cut for the other cheek. In plan, they look like detail 5 above. Now you're ready to make the double-cheeked plumb cut for irregular rafter A, and to take a break.

In practice, when the rough framing is going to be covered up by a ceiling, I generally trim this cut to fit. A perfect cut isn't necessary for structural integrity, and as always, time is of the essence. But a journeyman carpenter should know how to make this cut precisely if the rafters are going to be exposed to view.

I let the tails of these two rafters run wild past the wall. Once I've got the rest of the rafters in place, I use my level to determine the position of my tail cut. In this manner I can make sure that the fascia and gutters end up in the right place.

Irregular Hip B

These hips can be calculated mathematically, but to tell the truth I use stringlines to figure them out. I tack a nail in the top of the valley rafter to represent the centerline intersection of the valley and its neighboring hip. Then I run a string to the point at which the rafters are intersecting at the end of the ridge. I'll measure this distance to get the unadjusted length of the rafter, and while I'm at it I measure the distance from the stringline to the wall plate to get the depth of the seat cut.

To lay out the radically tapered tail cut on hip B, I need to know the angle the rafter makes with the front of the bay. Using the tangent method, I find it to be 35½°. From the plan view we see that the 45° valley and 35½° hip come together to form a 9½° angle (45° minus 35½°). The complement of 9½° is 80½°. I use this angle on my Speed Square to mark the tail cut. Once I adjust the cheek cut for the pitch of the rafter, I make the cut with a sharp handsaw. The only rafters left to install are the hip jacks.

Because I have 3 ft. from corner to common rafter, I center the jack at 1 ft. 6 in. You should have enough information now to figure out their rise, run, pitch, length, and cheek cuts.

Don Dunkley is a framing contractor working in California's central valley.

Shed-Dormer Retrofit

■ BY SCOTT McBRIDE

Growing up amid the post-war baby plantations of central Long Island, I got to see a lot of expand-as-you-go housing. One of my earliest memories is the sight of slightly dangerous-looking men, with hairy arms and sweaty faces, tearing the roof off our home. My parents had decided to add onto our modest Cape, and that meant building a shed dormer. The following spring, a neighbor came over to take measurements; his house and ours, you see, were identical, and he wanted to do the same thing to his place. Before long, all the houses in our subdivision had sprouted the same 14-ft.-long dormer.

Rivaled only by the finished basement, the enlarged and finished attic endures as the most practical way for the average suburban family to ease its growing pains. The shed dormer makes it possible to enlarge almost any attic space simply by flipping up the plane of the gable roof. Compared with the cost and complexity of a gable dormer, the shed dormer is a good choice where size and budget take precedence over looks.

Loading and Bearing

Once you're sure that the existing ceiling joists will support live floor loads, you have to consider the other structural aspects of adding a shed dormer. Removing all or part of the rafters on one side of a gable roof upsets its structural equilibrium. You're taking a stable, triangulated structure and turning it into a not-so-stable trapezoid. The downward and outward forces exerted by the remaining rafters are no longer neatly countered by opposing members. The dormer's framing system has to compensate for this lost triangulation. To understand how this happens, let's take a look at a dormer's structural anatomy. As shown in the drawing on p. 80, the inboard header transfers loading from the cripple rafters out to the trimmer rafters on either side of the dormer. The full-length trimmer rafters send this lateral thrust down to the joists. With the main roof load reapportioned around the dormer, the new roof is structurally able to stand on its own.

The shed dormer makes it possible to enlarge almost any attic space simply by flipping up the plane of the gable roof.

On low-pitched dormers, the roof sheathing acts as a sort of horizontal beam that reinforces the inboard header and helps transfer the lateral thrust of the main roof out to the trimmer rafters. As you increase the pitch of the dormer, you decrease the ability of the dormer roof to act as a horizontal beam. And the lateral force of the dormer rafters themselves will sometimes threaten to bow out the dormer face wall. The solution is to tie the main-roof rafters and dormer rafters together with ceiling joists. These act as collar ties, creating a modified version of the original gable triangle.

We also have to consider vertical loads. The dormer roof on the outboard side is supported by the dormer face wall, which is built either directly atop the exterior wall or slightly to the inside, where it bears on the attic floor joists. This second option leaves a small section of the original roof plane (called the apron) intact, and lets you retain the existing cornice and gutter. It also sets the dormer back a bit from the eaves line and visually reduces the weight of the addition.

Depending on the size of your floor joists, if the setback is more than one or

TIP

To lighten the load on the attic floor joists, install a header to the trimmer rafters.

Retrofit Framing Details

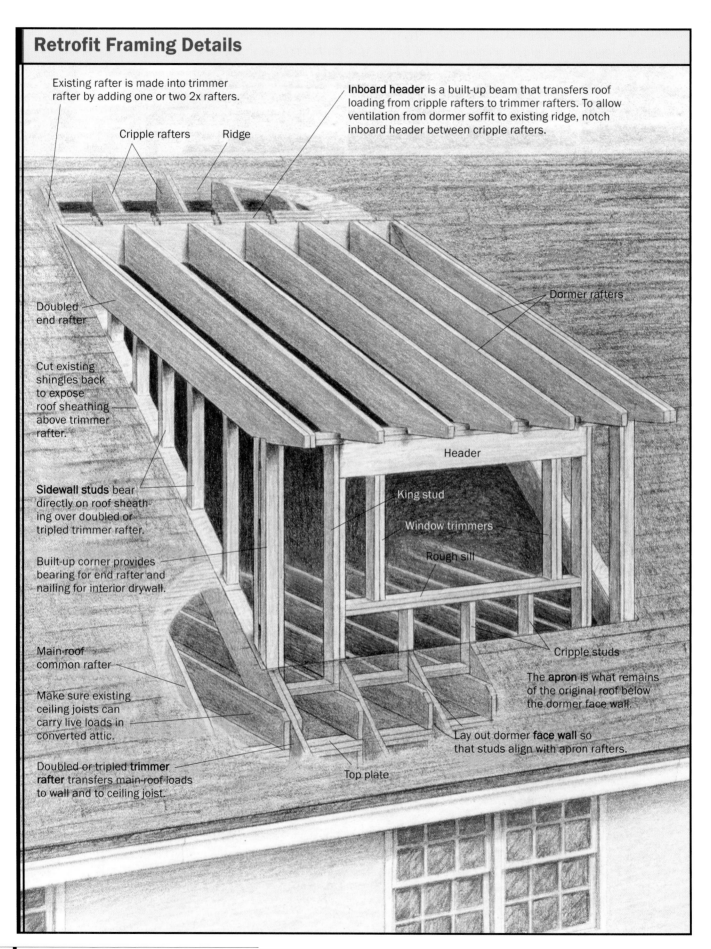

Existing rafter is made into trimmer rafter by adding one or two 2x rafters.

Cripple rafters

Ridge

Inboard header is a built-up beam that transfers roof loading from cripple rafters to trimmer rafters. To allow ventilation from dormer soffit to existing ridge, notch inboard header between cripple rafters.

Dormer rafters

Doubled end rafter

Cut existing shingles back to expose roof sheathing above trimmer rafter.

Header

Sidewall studs bear directly on roof sheathing over doubled or tripled trimmer rafter.

King stud

Window trimmers

Rough sill

Built-up corner provides bearing for end rafter and nailing for interior drywall.

Main-roof common rafter

Make sure existing ceiling joists can carry live loads in converted attic.

Cripple studs

The **apron** is what remains of the original roof below the dormer face wall.

Lay out dormer **face wall** so that studs align with apron rafters.

Doubled or tripled **trimmer rafter** transfers main-roof loads to wall and to ceiling joist.

Top plate

two feet, the load on the attic floor joists can become too great. To lighten this load, you should install a header to the trimmer rafters. In any case, this face wall will support a little more than half the weight of the dormer, depending on the roof pitch.

The other half of the dormer roof load usually rests on a large inboard header, which transmits the load through the trimmer rafters down to the exterior walls. To increase roof pitch and gain more headroom, the inboard header is frequently moved all the way up to the ridge of the main roof. If this ridge beam is made strong enough to carry roughly half the weight of the dormer roof and half the weight of the main roof, then it won't sag, and the rafters connected to it cannot spread apart at the plates. This allows the attic to have a cathedral ceiling.

If the ceiling is to be flat, the ceiling joists will prevent the roof from spreading, as mentioned earlier. In this case the ridge is nonstructural and can be made of lighter stuff.

If you don't use ceiling joists and go for a cathedral ceiling, the length of your dormer will depend upon the practical length of the inboard header or structural ridge beam. About 12 ft. to 16 ft. is typical. At this length, a triple 2x10 or 2x12 should make an adequate header, capable of carrying half the dormer roof load, plus the weight of any cripple rafters above it. If the 2xs in the built-up header are slightly offset from one another and the main roof pitch is steep enough, the header will not protrude below the ceiling. Sizes of all members should be checked by an engineer, architect, or building inspector.

If you're going to build a long dormer, you can support the header between the trimmer rafters with an intermediate rafter. Hidden inside a partition wall that runs perpendicular to the face wall, this rafter picks up the load of the headers, which can then be reduced in size.

Designing a Shed Dormer

Shed dormers may be so narrow as to accommodate only a window or two, or may run the entire length of the house. In the latter case, it is common to leave a strip of the main roof alongside the rake at each gable end (photo, p. 79).

The trickiest part of designing a dormer is getting the profile right. To find the correct position of the inboard header and the dormer face wall, begin by making a scale drawing of the existing roof. Then draw in the dormer that you have in mind. What you're trying to determine here are the height of the dormer's face wall, the pitch of its roof, and where these two planes will intersect the plane of the main roof.

When determining the height of the face wall, consider exterior appearance, interior headroom, and window heights. The roof pitch you choose will affect the kind of roofing. Shingles require at least a 4-in-12 pitch. A flatter pitch should be roofed with 90-lb. roll roofing. This usually isn't a visual problem because you can't see the flatter roof from the ground.

Preparation

Before you cut a big hole in your roof, you have to determine the location of the dormer from inside the attic. Lay some kind of temporary floor over the open joists to keep boots from going through ceilings and to keep trash out of the attic insulation.

You may want to use one of the existing rafters as a starting point and lay out the dormer from there. In this case the existing rafter becomes a trimmer rafter and will have to be doubled or possibly tripled to carry the load. This can be done before the roof is opened up.

Marking and Cutting the Roof

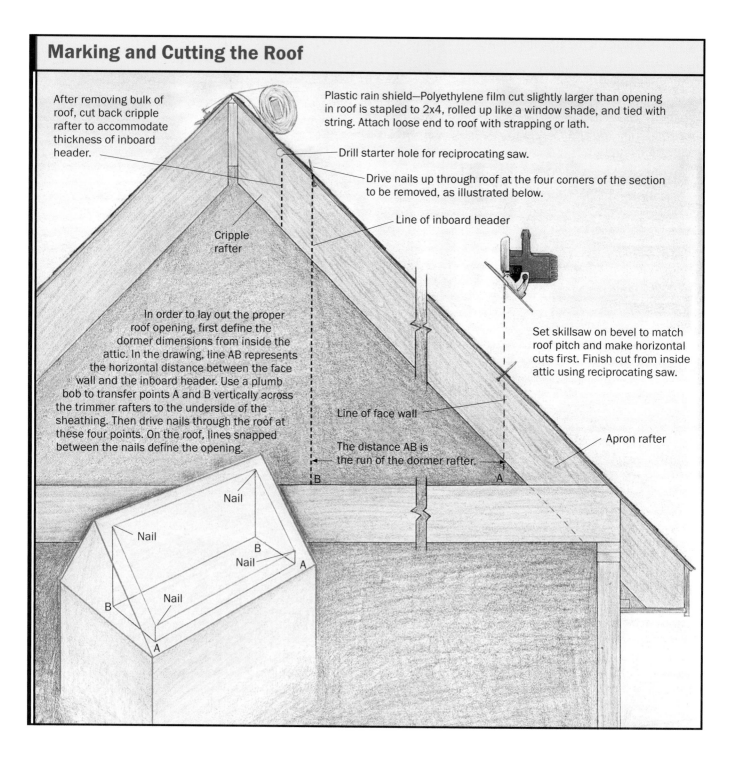

After removing bulk of roof, cut back cripple rafter to accommodate thickness of inboard header.

Plastic rain shield—Polyethylene film cut slightly larger than opening in roof is stapled to 2x4, rolled up like a window shade, and tied with string. Attach loose end to roof with strapping or lath.

Drill starter hole for reciprocating saw.

Drive nails up through roof at the four corners of the section to be removed, as illustrated below.

Line of inboard header

Cripple rafter

In order to lay out the proper roof opening, first define the dormer dimensions from inside the attic. In the drawing, line AB represents the horizontal distance between the face wall and the inboard header. Use a plumb bob to transfer points A and B vertically across the trimmer rafters to the underside of the sheathing. Then drive nails through the roof at these four points. On the roof, lines snapped between the nails define the opening.

Set skillsaw on bevel to match roof pitch and make horizontal cuts first. Finish cut from inside attic using reciprocating saw.

Line of face wall

The distance AB is the run of the dormer rafter.

Apron rafter

B   A

Nail

Nail

B

Nail   A

Nail

B

Nail

A

To lay out these extra trimmer rafters, measure the underside of an existing rafter from the heel of the plumb cut at the ridge down to the heel of the level cut at the plate. Transfer the respective angles with your T-bevel. These extra rafters don't support the cornice, so you don't have to cut a bird's mouth; just let the level cut run through. If a ceiling joist prevents the new rafters from reaching the plate, raise the level cut on the bottom of the rafters so they bear snugly on the top edge of the joist.

Now slide the additional rafters into the appropriate bays to make the trimmers. Any roofing nails protruding below the sheathing should be nipped off. Some persuasion may be necessary to bring the new rafter up tight against the old one. Spike the rafters together generously and toenail the new ones to the ridge and plate.

Now that you've defined the length of the dormer, you need to mark off the width. Begin by measuring from the outside of the exterior wall in to where you want the face wall (drawing, facing page). From here plumb a line up across the trimmer rafter and mark where this line intersects the roof. Now measure horizontally toward the ridge, from the proposed face wall to where you want the inboard header. Plumb another line up to the trimmer from here, and mark where it intersects the roof. This distance is the width of your dormer; it's also the run of the dormer rafter. Where these points (two on each set of trimmer rafters) touch the underside of the sheathing, drive four large nails up through the roof to mark the corners of the rectangular section you'll cut out from above. But before heading up to make the cuts, check for electrical wires, vent stacks, and anything else you don't want your skillsaw to run into.

Rigging

Since houses with steep roof pitches make the best candidates for dormers, you'll need good rigging. Set up staging along the eaves, extending a few feet past both sides of the dormer location. If a hoist or pulley can be rigged in conjunction with the scaffold, so much the better. To gain access along the sides of the dormer, a ladder can be hooked over the ridge, or roof brackets can be set up.

"What happens if it rains?" is the question most often asked by clients. If proper precautions are not taken while the house undergoes dormer surgery, a heavy rainstorm could cause thousands of dollars in damage.

Once you get up to the ridge, install an emergency rain shield—a piece of heavy polyethylene film wrapped around a 2x4 somewhat longer than the length of the dormer. On the ground, spread out a piece of the poly several feet longer than the

dormer and wide enough to reach from the ridge of the existing roof to the eaves. Staple one of the horizontal edges to the 2x4, and roll the sheet up like a window shade. Tie the roll with string, then carry it up to the roof and fasten its free edge to the ridge with wood lath or strapping. If it rains, cut the string and let the sheet unroll. The weight of the 2x4 hanging over the eaves will keep the poly tight, so it won't flap in the wind and so puddles won't develop.

Demolition

For cutting through the roof, you need a powerful skillsaw equipped with a nail-cutting blade. The heavy carbide tips on these blades are ground almost square, giving them the toughness needed to plow through asphalt, plywood, and miscellaneous nails all at once. Some manufacturers coat this type of blade with Teflon® to reduce friction. Eye protection is a must during this operation.

After snapping lines between the four nails you drove up through the roof, make the horizontal cuts first (there are only two of them and they're a little tougher to do). Set the skillsaw as deep as it will go, and set the saw's shoe to the plumb-cut angle of the main roof. Since you cannot safely plunge-cut with a skillsaw when it's set on an angle, start the cut with your drill and reciprocating saw. Then use a slow, steady feed on the skillsaw. Keep moving, because the weight of the saw will tend to push the downhill side of the sawblade against the work, generating extra friction. Be particularly alert to the possibility of kickback; your blade will be crashing into 8d sheathing nails now and then. And remember, you're up on a roof.

To make the vertical cuts, set the skillsaw back to 90° and start the cut on the uphill end. These cuts are easier because the weight of the saw helps pull it through the cut. All you have to do is slide down the roof behind it. If you have had experience plunge-cutting, then begin this way. Otherwise, start the cut

TIP

"What happens if it rains?" is the question most often asked by clients. Take proper precautions while the house undergoes dormer surgery; otherwise, a heavy rainstorm could cause thousands of dollars in damage.

Piggyback shed dormers. Shed dormers are often part of the original design on houses that have a gambrel roof. Here a second dormer was added on top of the first, probably to let more light into the room. The piggyback dormer also accommodates an air conditioner.

with the reciprocating saw, and finish with the skillsaw.

After the four outline cuts are done, make longitudinal cuts down the middle of each bay in the area to be removed. This divides the roof into manageable chunks. Before freeing these chunks by completing the cuts through the rafters, determine whether the remaining roof frame (the apron rafters below, and the cripple rafters above) need temporary support. If these pieces are short and well-nailed to the plate and ridge, they

will stay up by themselves. If not, shore them up temporarily with 2x4 braces.

Now use your reciprocating saw inside the attic to complete the cuts through the rafters. Have a couple of burly helpers hold up each section while you're working on it. A 10-ft. 2x8 rafter, 14 sq. ft. of sheathing, and several layers of roofing make these chunks very heavy. The safest way to lower them to the ground is with a strong rope that's wrapped around a sturdy mast.

After removing the bulk of the roof, the bottom ends of the cripple rafters must be cut back to accommodate the thickness of the inboard header, without cutting through the sheathing. Drill a ¾-in. starter hole at the top of the mark with a right-angle drill. Then cut straight down with the reciprocating saw.

To finish up the demolition, you'll need to cut back the roofing material to make way for the dormer sidewalls. Set the depth of the skillsaw so that it will cut through all the roof shingles, but will just graze the sheathing. Snap longitudinal lines on the roofing, located back from the inside faces of the trimmers a distance equal to the width of the dormer sidewall framing plus sheathing thickness, plus ½ in. for clearance. Slice through the roof shingles along these lines, and peel back the roofing to expose strips of decking above the trimmer rafters. The dormer sidewalls will be built up from these, with the inside edges of the studs flush with the inside faces of the trimmer rafters.

Wall Framing

Your next step will be to cut and lay out the plates for the face wall. In most situations, the bottom plate for the face wall will bear directly on the attic floor. You should lay out the face-wall framing so that the apron rafters will bear directly on the wall studs (aligning the framing in this way is called stacking).

In order to bring concentrated roof loads down safely onto the floor framing, window king studs also should be in line with the apron rafters or else be located over a joist. You can then frame inward to get the necessary rough-opening width. Or you can forget all this and just double the bottom plate to distribute the load safely.

Taking the scaled measurements from your drawings, transfer the header and sill lengths onto the plates. The various stud lengths will also come from your drawings. Be sure to locate the rough sill for the windows at least several inches above the apron to keep rain and melted snow from creeping in underneath.

Cut all the face-wall components and assemble them on the attic floor. Then raise and plumb the wall, bracing it temporarily if necessary.

Next you have to fill out the corners of the face wall with a combination of beveled sidewall studs and blocking, as shown in the drawing on p. 80. The tops of these studs will be flush with the top of the face wall, and will give bearing to the dormer end rafters. Begin by cutting oversized pieces with the pitch of the main roof cut on one end. Stand these in place and mark their tops flush with the top of the face wall. Cut and nail. This completes the face wall.

Roof Framing

The shed-dormer rafter is laid out just like any common rafter. The only differences are the generally lower pitch, and the fact that its plumb cut bears against a header instead of a ridge board. There are several ways to determine rafter length. I lay out the bird's mouth first, and then step off the rafter length with a large pair of dividers. After marking the plumb cut at the ridge, lay out the rafter tail according to the soffit and fascia details from your elevation drawings. Then carefully cut out the rafter pattern.

Turning to the roof, first nail the inboard header to the trimmers. Joist hangers won't work in this situation because you'll want to offset the 2xs like stair steps, starting each one slightly above or below the next in order to fit the slope of the roof. Instead, just toenail each piece in place with plenty of 16d commons, and then spike them to each other.

Have a couple of burly helpers hold up each section of roof while you're completing the cuts through the rafters.

Roofing and Flashing Details

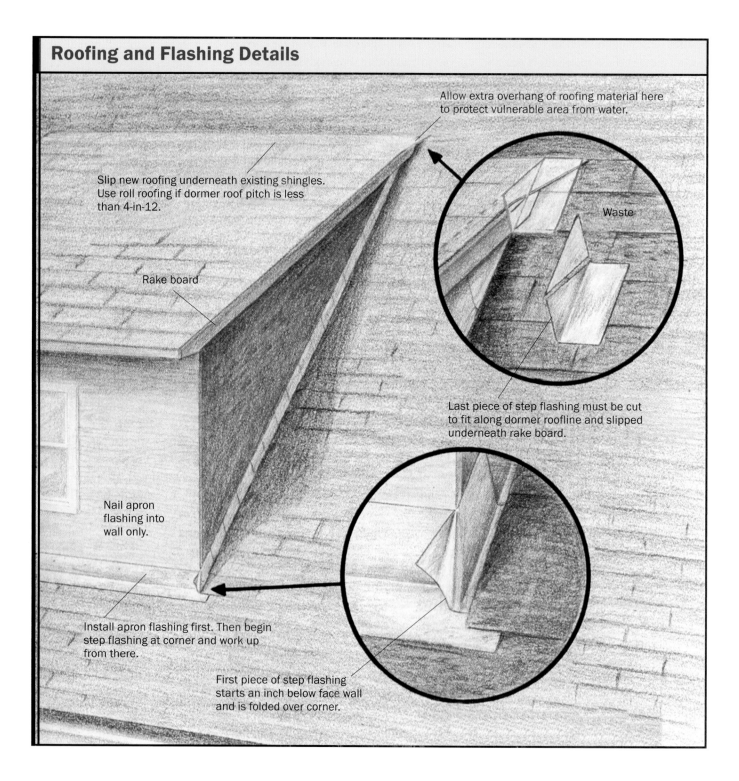

Allow extra overhang of roofing material here to protect vulnerable area from water.

Slip new roofing underneath existing shingles. Use roll roofing if dormer roof pitch is less than 4-in-12.

Rake board

Waste

Last piece of step flashing must be cut to fit along dormer roofline and slipped underneath rake board.

Nail apron flashing into wall only.

Install apron flashing first. Then begin step flashing at corner and work up from there.

First piece of step flashing starts an inch below face wall and is folded over corner.

Now try the rafter pattern at several different locations along the top plate of the face wall. If all is well, use the pattern to cut the rest of the rafters and nail them in place. The spacing of the rafters should align with the face-wall studs in the same way the studs align with the floor joists. The end rafters will have to be retrimmed directly on the roof instead of on the header. Place one of the pattern-cut rafters in position, up against the trimmer rafter, and mark the roofline. After cutting, double the end rafters to provide nailing for drywall, or spike a 2x on the flat with its bottom face flush with the bottom edge of the end rafter.

The dormer sidewall studs are framed directly from the main roof up to the dormer's end rafters, without any plates. As with the corners of the face wall, begin by cutting oversized pieces with the pitch of the main roof cut on one end. Then stand the pieces in place and mark where they meet the dormer end rafter, cut along the mark, and nail them up. These studs diminish in a regular progression, like gable studs, as they approach the ridge. If you don't want to mark each one in place, just mark the first two and measure the difference between them. This measurement is their common difference, and you can use it to calculate the diminishing lengths of the remaining studs.

Closing Up

A few points on exterior finish are worth mentioning. Before decking the dormer roof, use a shingle ripper to remove nails in the first course of roof shingles above the dormer. This allows the dormer roofing material to be slipped underneath the existing shingles. If you install the sheathing first, the lower pitch of the dormer roof will interfere with the handle of the shingle ripper.

Flashing a shed dormer is relatively simple. As shown in the drawing on the facing page, the apron is flashed first, then the dormer sidewalls are step-flashed. Use a 6-in.-wide length of flashing along the apron, creased in half so that 3 in. of flashing runs up the dormer face wall and 3 in. extends over the apron shingles. Nail the face-wall side only. At the corners of the face wall, let the apron flashing run a few inches past the dormer sidewall. Slit the flashing vertically along the corner of the dormer, and push the overhanging vertical fin down flat on the main roof.

Overlap the apron flashing with the first piece of step flashing, where the dormer sidewall meets the main roof extend the step flashing down at least an inch past the face wall, and fold the vertical fin down and back on an angle. This will carry rainwater safely past the corner. You'll have to relieve the back of the corner board to fit over this first piece of step flashing.

Continue the step flashing all the way up the sidewall, slipping one piece of bent step flashing under the end of each roof shingle course, and pressing the other side up against the wall sheathing. Don't nail the step flashing into the roof; nail it to the sidewall only.

The rake board is usually furred out with a piece of 5/4 spruce so the siding can be slipped underneath. Where the dormer rake board dies into the main roof, the uppermost piece of step flashing is trimmed on an angle so that it can fit up behind the rake board and tight against the furring. Give the dormer roofing a little extra overhang here to help divert water from this sensitive spot.

Vents in the dormer soffit are a good idea. They prevent condensation in the dormer roof insulation as well as ice damming at the eaves. Since the inboard header blocks the flow of warm air at the tops of the roof bays, cut some notches across the top of the header in each bay or recess the top edge of the header slightly below the tops of the dormer rafters. If you're insulating between the rafters (instead of the ceiling joists), you'll need some spacers to create an airflow channel between the roof sheathing and the insulation. This allows some airflow from the dormer soffit vent to the ridge vent or gable-end louvers.

Scott McBride *is a contributing editor of* Fine Homebuilding *and the author of* Build Like a Pro™: Windows and Doors, *published by The Taunton Press.*

Vents in the dormer soffit are a good idea to prevent condensation in the dormer roof insulation as well as ice damming at the eaves.

Raising an Eyebrow

■ BY JAMES DOCKER

Eyebrow dormers had their American heyday during the late 19th century, when they turned up on the elaborate roofs of Shingle-style Victorian and Richardsonian Romanesque houses. Tucked between the conical towers, spire-like chimneys, and abundant gables that distinguish these buildings, the little eyebrows provided a secondary level of detail to the roof and some much needed daylight to upstairs rooms and attics.

The roof cutters of that era could probably lay out an eyebrow dormer during a coffee break, but for a contemporary West Coast carpenter such as myself (well versed in shear walls, production framing, and remodeling techniques), framing an eyebrow dormer presented an out-of-the-ordinary challenge.

The setting for this dormer project was a rambling Tudor house in Atherton, California. The owners were adding a garage and remodeling several portions of the building, including a dilapidated barnlike recreation room next to the swimming pool. The roof of the house was covered with cedar shingles, and at the eaves and gable ends, curved shingles gave the roof a thatched look. Eyebrow dormers, rising by way of gentle curves

from the plane of the 8-in-12 roofs, would look right at home on the house.

My job was to install five of them in the garage roof and a single larger eyebrow dormer in the roof of the recreation room. The garage ceiling would remain unfinished, so I didn't need to worry about providing backing for drywall or plaster. I would, however, have to solve that problem in the recreation room. The garage dormers required a lower level of finish while presenting the same conceptual problems, so I decided to build them first.

Rafter-Type Eyebrow

By the time I got on the job, contractor Dave Tsukushi had already taken delivery of the windows for the garage roof. They were arched, single-glazed units available off-the-shelf from Pozzi® Wood Windows. The windows were 64 in. wide by 24 in. tall, and had 4-in.-wide frames made of pine. The arched frames were quite sturdy, so we decided to incorporate them as part of the structure. We faced them with ¾-in. ACX plywood, which would serve as a vertical surface for attaching the rafters, as well as backing for a stucco finish (top photo, p. 90). At the top of the arch, this plywood

Undulating courses of cedar shingles wrap over the warped contours of these eyebrow dormers on a Tudor-style house in Atherton, California. The solo dormer (left) lets light into the recreation room, while the others illuminate the garage (below).

Plywood face frames screwed to arched window frames support the ends of the 2x4 rafters. The rafters are on 4-in. centers and are parallel to one another. Note the uphill ends of the rafters. The outside and inside corners touch the base and determine its shape.

Before the window and the rafters are installed, a bell-shaped base sheet is affixed to the roof deck. The next step will be to cut away the decking inside the base.

face frame is 3¾ in. wider than the window frame. This dimension accommodates the 22½° plumb cut of a 2x4 rafter on a 5-in-12 slope—the pitch of our dormer. I screwed the face frame to the first window; then I braced it firmly on the roof, exactly on its layout between the roof trusses.

An arched window 2 ft. high with a base about 5 ft. wide makes a pretty tight curve for the dormer roof sheathing to follow. To make sure the curves stayed smooth and to ensure plenty of backing for the plywood, I decided to put my 2x4 rafters on 4-in. centers. I laid out their centerlines on the base of the window, and then used a level held plumb to transfer them to the arched portion of the face frame. Next I got out the string.

The Luxury of Full Scale

Normally I make detailed drawings of unusual framing assemblies to familiarize myself with the geometry involved while still sitting on terra firma. This first dormer proved to be an exception to that rule, as I had the luxury of mocking it up on the garage roof. Still, clambering around on an 8-in-12 roof deck isn't everybody's idea of fun, so I would recommend doing a detailed drawing of the dormer's essential components, and then using it to scale the lengths and angles (more on this in a minute).

The opening in the roof made by an eyebrow dormer is bell-shaped in plan (photo, left), with the bottom of the bell corresponding to the base of the window. Finding the shape of the bell became the next task.

First I tacked a couple of sheets of ½-in. ACX plywood to the roof deck (one over the other) so that their right edges were aligned with the centerline of the dormer. I specified plywood with an A side for all the plywood parts of the dormers (except for the sheathing) because it's much easier to draw accurate layout lines on a smooth, knot-free

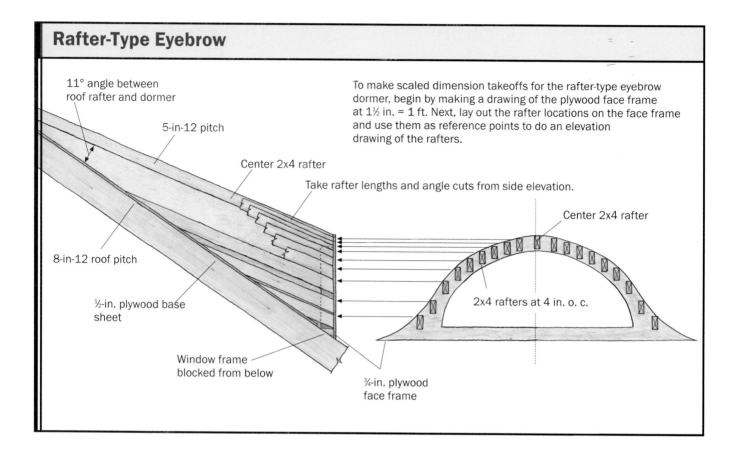

Rafter-Type Eyebrow

11° angle between roof rafter and dormer

5-in-12 pitch

Center 2x4 rafter

Take rafter lengths and angle cuts from side elevation.

8-in-12 roof pitch

½-in. plywood base sheet

Window frame blocked from below

¾-in. plywood face frame

To make scaled dimension takeoffs for the rafter-type eyebrow dormer, begin by making a drawing of the plywood face frame at 1½ in. = 1 ft. Next, lay out the rafter locations on the face frame and use them as reference points to do an elevation drawing of the rafters.

Center 2x4 rafter

2x4 rafters at 4 in. o. c.

expanse of plywood than it is on a bumpy C or D side.

Then I cut a 2-ft. length of 2x4 with a 5-in-12 plumb cut on one end to act as a dummy rafter and rested the cut end on the top of the window frame. I held a string flush to the top edge of the dummy rafter, using a helper to hold it at the uphill end. This stringline represented the top of the center rafter, and its intersection at the roof was marked. Then the stringline-and-mark process was repeated for each rafter positioned to the left of center. By connecting the marks with a smooth curve, I had the outside line of the bell. To find the inside line of the bell, I measured the angle between the string and the roof deck. This angle (11˚) represented the cut needed on the bottom of the dormer rafters where they intersect the garage roof. Because all the rafters are at the same pitch and parallel to one another, this cut is the same for all the rafters. By making a sample cut on a short length of 2x4, I simply placed the tapered

end on each rafter layout line and marked the inside corners. Connecting the dots gave me the inside of the bell curve. Because the rafter layouts are symmetrical, the bell-shaped base for half of the dormer is the mirror image of the other half. Therefore, half of one base is all the layout template needed for one dormer. The same applies to the rafters. Once I had them measured and cut for half of the first dormer, I had templates for all the rest, allowing me to cut the parts quickly for all five dormers.

All this string-holding worked okay. But if I were to do this again, I'd do a drawing at a scale of 1½ in. to 1 ft. showing the elevation of the window from two vantage points (drawing, above). At this scale, it would be easy to make dimension and angle takeoffs for the lengths of the rafters and the angle at which they intersect the roof and the face frame. Then I'd use the rafters instead of the stringlines to figure out the bell shape of the plywood plate.

TIP

Specify plywood with an A side for all the plywood parts of the dormers (except for the sheathing). It's much easier to draw accurate layout lines on a smooth, knot-free expanse of plywood than it is on a bumpy C or D side.

Assembly and Sheathing

Once the plywood plates were cut out, we screwed them to the roof deck with galvanized drywall screws. Then we cut out the decking on the interior side of the base sheet, and screwed the eyebrow rafters to the plate and the face frame.

When one of the dormers had all its rafters, we draped 30-lb. felt over half of it and trimmed the felt along the valley formed by the intersection of the garage roof and the side of the dormer. This gave us the pattern we needed for marking cutlines on the ⅜-in. CDX plywood sheathing.

Bending a sheet of plywood over a radius this tight while holding it on the layout can be daunting—especially on a steep roof—so I wanted to prebend the largest pieces. Shallow kerfs on the underside of the plywood would have allowed it to bend more easily, but the structure of the dormers is visible from below so I wanted to avoid kerfs. Instead, I made a simple bending form out of a sheet of plywood with some 2x4 cleats nailed to the long edges. Then I stuffed several of ⅜-in. plywood sheets between the cleats, soaking each one liberally with the garden hose. Left in the form for a couple of days, the sheets took on a distinct curve, making them easier to bend over the rafters. Each dormer has one layer of ⅜-in. plywood affixed to the framing with 1-in. staples. We left the tops of the rafters unbeveled, but added beveled strips for better bearing where the sheets abut one another.

The garage roof had skip sheathing atop its decking to give the cedar shingles some breathing space. We carried the skip sheathing over each dormer by stapling a double layer of 6-in.-wide redwood benderboard (⁵⁄₁₆ in. thick) on top of the plywood. Because the roofers had woven layers of shingles together with very little exposure to form the valleys (bottom photo, p. 89), we didn't need to worry about valley flashing.

After the Rafters, the Ribs

Unlike the multiple eyebrows on the garage roof, the single eyebrow atop the pool house had to have a finished ceiling underneath it. I decided that this extra wrinkle warranted another approach to the eyebrow's structure. Granted, you could hang blocking and furring strips from the bottom of a rafter-framed eyebrow to make a smooth transition from a flat ceiling plane to one with an arch, but why not make the bottom of the eyebrow structure conform as closely as possible to the shape of the arched portion of the ceiling? To that end, I worked up a full-scale drawing of the dormer (drawing, facing page) on the recreation-room floor.

The window hadn't yet been ordered for this eyebrow, allowing me to design the arch from scratch. I made it long and low, taking the bulk of its face frame from a 10-ft. sheet of ¾-in. plywood. The short reverse-curve valley returns at each end were made of scabbed-on pieces of plywood (photo, facing page).

The ribs are on 16-in. centers, and their bottoms are cut at an 8-in-12 pitch to match the roof slope. As the individual ribs step up the roof, their overall depth decreases along with their width. Meanwhile, their arc at the top remains the same as that of the face frame. By taking direct measurements off the full-scale drawing, I got the overall depth of each rib. Then I measured down on the centerline of the window face frame to find the perpendicular baseline to read the width of each rib. To add a little extra complexity to the project, I had to increase the depth of the web of each rib in a sequential manner. This allowed the arched portion of the ceiling to make its transition into the cathedral ceiling without crowding the ridge (photo, p. 95).

I made all the parts for the rib-type dormer out of ¾-in. plywood. The face frame is a single layer, the built-up window frame has five layers, and each rib has three layers.

Rather than adjust the ribs on the roof, the author brought the roof to the workspace. Temporarily tacked on this 8-in-12 worktable, the corners of the rib bases are noted on the plywood to generate the bell-shaped base. The paper pattern will be used to cut out the plywood sheathing.

Rib-Type Eyebrow

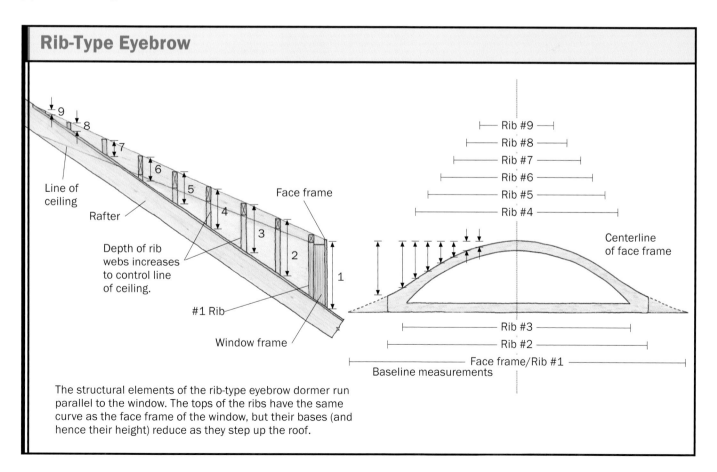

9
8
7
6
5
4
3
2
1

Line of ceiling

Rafter

Face frame

Depth of rib webs increases to control line of ceiling.

#1 Rib

Window frame

Rib #9
Rib #8
Rib #7
Rib #6
Rib #5
Rib #4

Centerline of face frame

Rib #3
Rib #2
Face frame/Rib #1
Baseline measurements

The structural elements of the rib-type eyebrow dormer run parallel to the window. The tops of the ribs have the same curve as the face frame of the window, but their bases (and hence their height) reduce as they step up the roof.

The bell-shaped base of the rib dormer rests on rafters that will soon be headed off and trimmed back.

Here you can see how the two rafters at the top, now cantilevered over a new ridge beam, have been cut back at a taper to keep them out of the arched ceiling plane. To their right, an angled doubler picks up the weight of the ribs bearing on the base sheet. Benderboard strips backed by 2x blocking define the curve of the arched ceiling.

Rib number 1 is screwed to the back of the window frame.

Working with a full-scale drawing made for accurate and speedy work. But the pieces were large and cumbersome, and temporarily tacking them to the roof to figure out the shape of the base didn't sound like any fun at all. I probably could have used the full-scale elevation drawing to extrapolate its shape, but whenever I have to deal with unusual concepts, like sections of cones on inclined planes, I take comfort in three-dimensional models.

While regarding the cavernous interior of the recreation room, a solution occurred to me. Why not build a mockup of the roof, with one end of the rafters firmly planted on the recreation-room floor? Within an hour, I had a fake roof in place. I used the plywood that would eventually become the base sheet for its sheathing.

As each rib was cut out according to direct measurement takeoffs, I tacked its base to the fake roof and braced it plumb with a temporary alignment spine (photo, p. 93). Once I had all the ribs tacked to the mockup, I marked the inside and outside points where their bases engaged the plywood. These points gave me the reference marks I needed to make the bell-shaped base for the ribs. After taking the ribs down, I drove 8d nails at each mark, leaving enough of the nails exposed to act as stops. Then I used a ¼-in. by 1½-in. strip of straight-grained redwood benderboard held against the protruding nails to generate the curve for the base sheet.

The base sheet tucks into a bay between a pair of new timber-framed trusses (top left photo). Unlike the installation of the rafter-type dormers, this one went into a roof that hadn't been planned with an eyebrow dormer in mind. This meant that some rafters had to be removed, and their loads picked up and transferred to new structural members.

A plaster finish on the arched ceiling flows into the drywall covering the plane of the rafters.

Blocking and Benderboard

Before I took apart the mocked-up structure of the dormer, I made a rosin-paper pattern to guide the cutting of the plywood sheathing. Like the pattern for the dormers on the garage, this one could be flopped to be the pattern for the other side of the dormer.

Assembling the ribs began from the bottom up. With the face frame and its accompanying arches firmly attached to the base sheet and diagonally braced plumb, all the succeeding ribs were quickly placed on their layout marks. They were then decked with a single layer of ½-in. plywood. As before, I built up skip sheathing over the top of the eyebrow with two layers of ³⁄₁₆-in. by 6-in. benderboard.

Picking up the loads of the removed rafters and carrying the curves of the ribs into the plane of the ceiling was the next task. Our engineer recommended using a couple of doubled 2x8s as support for the legs of the base sheet. These doublers run diagonally from the ridge beam to the top chords of the new timber-framed trusses (bottom photo, facing page). This photo also shows the finicky blocking that it took to pick up the unsupported edges of plywood sheathing and to carry the arc of the eyebrow into plane with the rafters. Benderboard was also useful for this task. In places, I was able to extend the curve from a rib to the rafters with a strip of benderboard and then fill in the remaining gaps with solid pieces of blocking shaped to fit.

The ends of the benderboard abut the edges of the drywall that cover the flat parts of the ceiling. At the transition to the curve, expanded metal lath was stapled over the benderboard, and the junction between the flat ceiling and the eyebrow's arch feathered with plaster to make an invisible seam.

James Docker is a building designer and general contractor living in San Carlos, California.

Sources

Pozzi Wood Windows
P.O. Box 5249
Bend, OR 97708
(800) 821-1016
www.pozzi.com

Framing a Bay-Window Roof

■ BY SCOTT McBRIDE

For as long as architects have been draw-ing bay windows, carpenters have been scratching their heads about framing the roofs. Victorian builders sometimes got around the problem by letting two-story bays die into a projection of the main roof above. Tract builders in the 1950s did like-wise by tucking bay windows under over-hanging second floors or wide eaves.

When a bay bumps out on its own, how-ever, it needs a miniature hip roof to keep out the elements. Because the corners of bay windows aren't square, neither is the roof above, and figuring the rafter cuts isn't straightforward. I've built many of these roofs and have worked out a system that does the job without guesswork.

Roofs on Site-Built or Manufactured Bays Are Much the Same

The skeleton of a bay roof breaks down into two parts (drawing, p. 98). The first part is the cornice, an assembly of horizontal look-outs tied together by subfascias. (A subfascia will receive a finished material, in this case aluminum coil stock. If you're planning to install a painted wood fascia, you can sub-stitute the finished fascia material for the subfascia.) A horizontal ledger carries the lookouts where they attach to the building.

The common rafters for the middle roof, hip rafters, and jack rafters comprise the sec-ond part of the skeleton. The side roofs also require sloped ledgers to support the sheath-ing where it meets the building.

Bays can be site-framed or manufactured units. When the walls of a bay are framed on site, the horizontal lookouts double as ceiling joists. In that case, the lookouts bear directly on the wall's top plates.

When I'm installing a manufactured bay, as I did for this article, the bay's plywood headboard provides the ceiling. With the bay installed, I screw through the headboard to affix 2x4 plates above, parallel with the bay's outside edges. I nail a second plate atop the first. This step makes room for a 3-in. frieze above the windows, which I think looks better than having the fascia

A sturdy scaffold makes for efficient bay-roof construction. The walk-board height allows work to be done at waist level. The boards behind serve as a workbench, saving a lot of climbing up and down.

Two Distinct Assemblies Comprise a Bay Roof

The lower portion, or cornice, rests on the bay's walls, or on 2x4 plates fastened to the headboard if it's a manufactured unit. The rafters that form the roof's upper portion fasten to the cornice members and to the house wall.

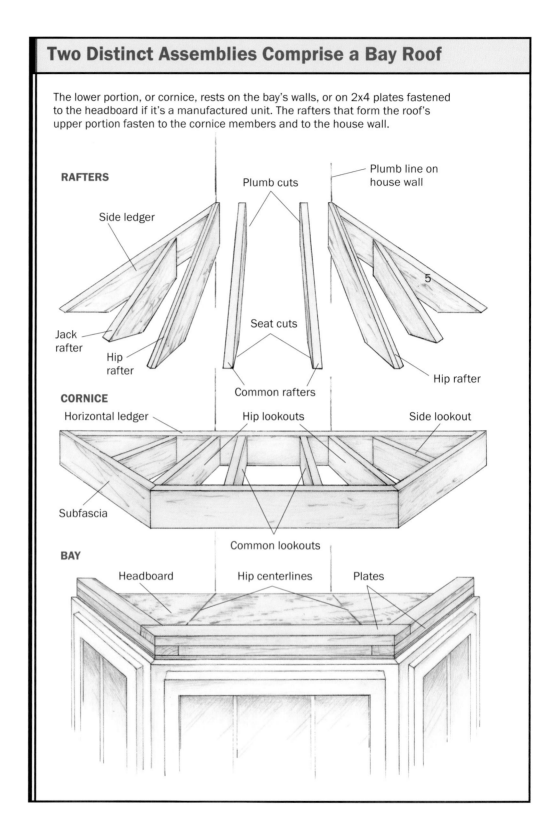

RAFTERS

Plumb cuts

Plumb line on house wall

Side ledger

Jack rafter

Hip rafter

Seat cuts

Common rafters

Hip rafter

CORNICE

Horizontal ledger

Hip lookouts

Side lookout

Subfascia

Common lookouts

BAY

Headboard

Hip centerlines

Plates

directly above the glass. Raising the overhang lets in more light and provides room for insulation, which must usually be installed before the roof is sheathed. As a final plus, adding plates to the headboard provides a meatier surface for nailing the lookouts.

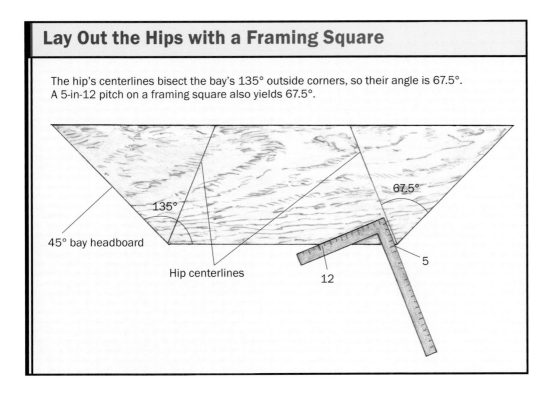

The hip's centerlines bisect the bay's 135° outside corners, so their angle is 67.5°. A 5-in-12 pitch on a framing square also yields 67.5°.

45° bay headboard

135°

Hip centerlines

67.5°

12

5

There Are No Rectangles in a Hipped Bay Roof

A frequent mistake is framing the middle roof as a rectangle, using common rafters as hips. This error makes the side roofs steeper than the middle roof. The result looks clunky, and the disparity in pitch complicates the cornice details.

Bisecting the bay angle with the hip shapes the middle roof as a trapezoid and also ensures that the middle roof and the side roofs will be equally pitched.

Before attaching the plates, I draw the centerline of each hip on the headboard, extending the line all the way to the house. To find the centerlines, it helps to realize that the angle encompassed by a bay window is not its nominal angle, in this case 45°, but rather its supplement. (An angle plus its supplement equals 180°) So the outer corners of a 45° bay each encompass an angle of 135° (drawing above). The hips bisect these angles, so the hip centerline angle for a 45° bay is half of 135°, or 67.5°. The other common

bay angle is 30°. The techniques in this article work on 30° bays, or bays of any angle for that matter, but you'll have to adjust the angles accordingly.

To lay out the hip centerline accurately, I use a framing square. Conveniently, a 5:12 angle on a framing square is equal to 67.5°, the hip angle of a 45° bay. I place 5 on the apex of the bay's angle, 12 on either the front or side edge of the bay, and mark on the 5 side. Doubling 5:12 to 10:24 provides even greater accuracy.

I pencil plumb lines on the house wall where the hip centerlines intersect it. These plumb lines serve as references for locating the hip lookouts and hip rafters.

Lookouts Form a Map for the Rafters to Follow

After plating, I install the 2x6 horizontal ledger. Its ends function as lookouts, supporting the subfascias where they die into the building. I cut the ledger's ends to match the bay's angle and its length to support the subfascia at the proper overhang.

Next come the common lookouts. I usually start the layout in the bay's middle and work outward. By centering either a lookout or the space between two lookouts, I can lay out the cornice so that a common lookout ends up close to each hip. In this way, I can usually avoid having to place a jack lookout between the last common and the hip. Because I position a rafter over each lookout, this consideration also eliminates a jack rafter.

Common lookouts are cut square on both ends, but I miter the side lookouts at 45° where they hit the ledger. In both cases, I find their length by measuring the distance from the ledger to the outside of the plate, then adding the overhang less the subfascia. I nail the common and side lookouts to the ledger before cutting the hip lookouts.

To find the length of the hip lookouts, I cut a 22½° miter on the inboard end of an oversize piece of lookout stock. I tack this stock in position above the hip centerline and use a straightedge to project lines from the ends of the common and side lookouts. These lines should cross the end of the hip to form a 22½° miter. I trim and permanently install the hip lookouts. Hanging the subfascias completes the cornice frame.

Drawing the Roof First Takes the Guesswork from the Rafter Angles

The rafters of a bay roof contain a surprising variety of angles. To understand these angles and make a more accurate job, I sometimes draw them on a sheet of plywood. This process is called graphic development. Bay roofs are generally small enough to draw full scale, but the same process can be used to develop angles for larger roofs by drawing at a reduced scale.

Geometric drawings may seem beyond the call of duty for the average carpenter, but the alternative was described to me succinctly by one of my backwoods buddies: "We just cut on 'er till she fits."

I start the graphic development by drawing a half-plan that shows the outside of the bay's cornice (top drawing, facing page). The first line to be added to the half-plan is the run of the hip, AB, drawn as it was on the headboard. Next, I draw the run of a common rafter, BC, perpendicular to the house wall.

The next move is establishing the slope of the common rafters. Sometimes I know the pitch, such as the 8-in-12 pitch shown here. In that case, I lay out the common-rafter slope with a framing square (line CD in center drawing, facing page).

Other times, I want the roof of the bay to top out at a particular elevation, such as the bottom of a window or the bottom of a clapboard. To find the slope of the common rafters in these cases, I measure the rise from the top of the lookouts to the desired elevation. On the drawing, I place D this distance from B.

To find the slope of the hip, I swing an arc from D and centered on B until it crosses a line raised perpendicular to AB. The point of intersection is E, and BE represents the rise of the hip. The idea behind swinging an arc is to transfer the rise of the common, BD, to the rise of the hip, BE, because the common and the hip rise the same distance.

The side ledger also rises the same distance as the common and the hip. To find it, extend line BC until it intersects the arc at F. BF is the rise of the ledger, and it corresponds to the plumb line drawn on the house's wall. FG is the ledger's slope (bottom drawing, facing page).

Full-scale graphic development provides all the information you need to make the plumb and seat cuts as well as lengths of the rafters. Bird's mouths aren't required for any of the seat cuts; the rafters simply sit on top of the lookouts and are nailed in place.

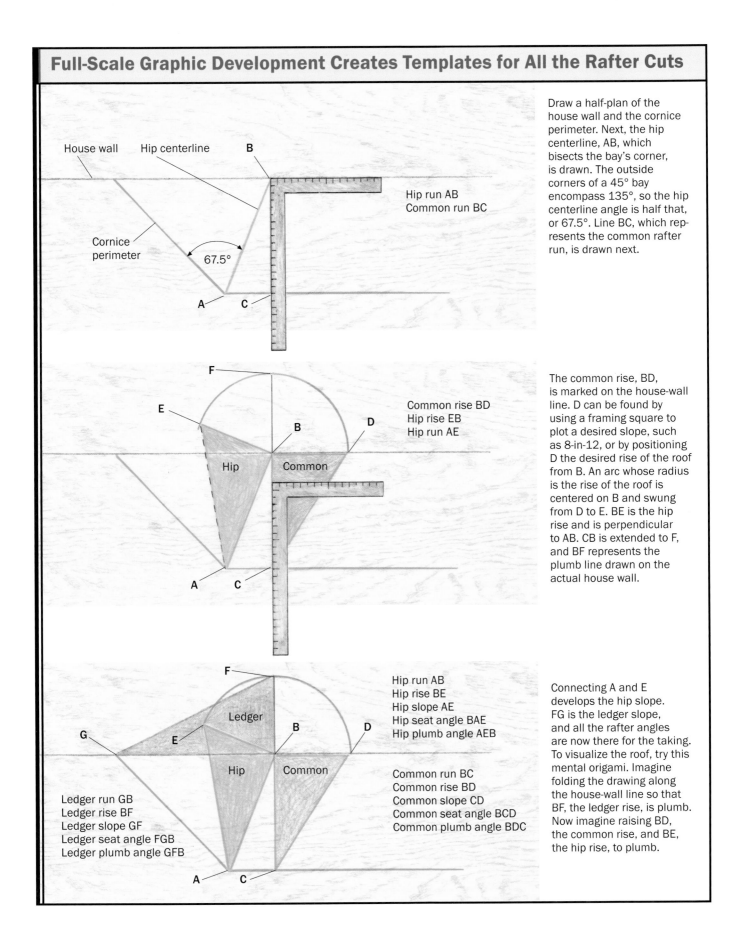

Draw a half-plan of the house wall and the cornice perimeter. Next, the hip centerline, AB, which bisects the bay's corner, is drawn. The outside corners of a 45° bay encompass 135°, so the hip centerline angle is half that, or 67.5°. Line BC, which represents the common rafter run, is drawn next.

House wall
Hip centerline
B

Hip run AB
Common run BC

Cornice perimeter
67.5°
A   C

The common rise, BD, is marked on the house-wall line. D can be found by using a framing square to plot a desired slope, such as 8-in-12, or by positioning D the desired rise of the roof from B. An arc whose radius is the rise of the roof is centered on B and swung from D to E. BE is the hip rise and is perpendicular to AB. CB is extended to F, and BF represents the plumb line drawn on the actual house wall.

F
E
B   D

Common rise BD
Hip rise EB
Hip run AE

Hip   Common
A   C

Connecting A and E develops the hip slope. FG is the ledger slope, and all the rafter angles are now there for the taking. To visualize the roof, try this mental origami. Imagine folding the drawing along the house-wall line so that BF, the ledger rise, is plumb. Now imagine raising BD, the common rise, and BE, the hip rise, to plumb.

F

Hip run AB
Hip rise BE
Hip slope AE
Hip seat angle BAE
Hip plumb angle AEB

Ledger
G   E   B   D

Hip   Common

Common run BC
Common rise BD
Common slope CD
Common seat angle BCD
Common plumb angle BDC

Ledger run GB
Ledger rise BF
Ledger slope GF
Ledger seat angle FGB
Ledger plumb angle GFB

A   C

Aligning the Hips and Ledgers with the Roof Plane

Full-scale graphic development generates two-dimensional templates for all the rafters of a bay roof. When cut, however, edges of the three-dimensional hips and ledgers will protrude above the roof plane unless the rafters are dropped or beveled.

BEVELING

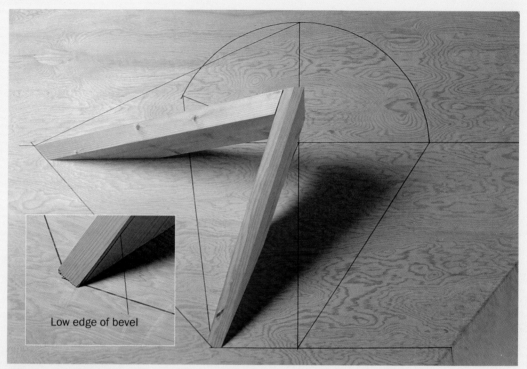

Low edge of bevel

With the rafter stock held in place on the graphic development, the low edge of the bevel is easily marked (inset). The high point of the hip's bevel is the center of the rafter. The ledger's high point is the upper edge that contacts the house.

DROPPING

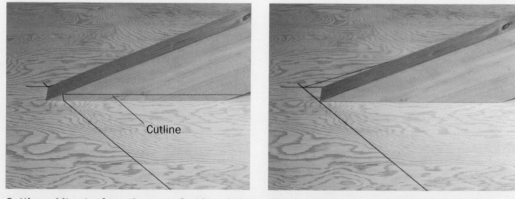

Cutline

Cutting a bit extra from the seat of a hip or ledger will align it with the roof plane. A plumb line raised where the held-in-place rafter intersects the bay's perimeter (left) shows how much to cut off the rafter (right). Unlike beveled rafters, sheathing contacts only the dropped rafters' edge.

Dropping or Beveling the Hip and Side Ledgers

Graphic development outlines the entire top surface of the common rafters, but the hips and side ledgers are more complex. The slope lines from the graphic development are one-dimensional representations of the centerline at the top of the hip and of the top edge of the side ledger that hits the house. The actual rafters are, of course, three-dimensional. The corners of a hip rafter or side ledger will protrude above the adjoining roof planes unless some adjustment is made (sidebar, facing page).

One way to make the adjustment is to drop the hip or ledger so that just the corners align with the roof plane. Cutting a little extra from the seat cut does this alignment. An alternative is to bevel, or back, the top edge of the rafter so that the edge is in plane with the roof. Backing is nice if you've got a table saw handy, but dropping works just as well.

To find the drops, I cut scrap blocks with the same seat cut as the hip and the ledger. I place the blocks in position on the developed drawing, straddling the hip centerline or, for the side ledger, on the wall line. The hip line on the drawing represents the rafter's center, so the center of the scrap block must align with the apex of the cornice angle. For the ledger, the line represents its inward edge, so the inner corner of the scrap must land on the intersection of the house and the cornice. I then draw plumb lines on the scraps, starting from where the blocks intersect the cornice's edges. The height of these lines is the drop to be deducted from the seat cut of the hip or of the side ledger.

If you want to bevel the rafters, you need to go one step further. From where the block touches the edge of the bay, draw a line on the block parallel to its top edge. This line is the low side of the backing bevel. The center of the hip or the opposing corner of the ledger represents the high side.

Raising the Roof

If a band or rim joist backs up the sheathing where the commons top out, as is often the case, the common rafters can be nailed directly to the sheathing. If not, it's a good idea to shorten the hips and commons by a horizontal distance of 1½ in., and hang them on a 2x ledger. The ledger ends line up on the plumb lines I raised earlier from the hip centerlines drawn atop the bay. The ledger's top will have to be dropped or beveled so that it's in plane with the rafters.

If there is to be a horizontal ledger for the common rafters, I install it and the side ledgers now. If there is no horizontal ledger, I install the hip first, centering it on the plumb line I raised earlier from the bay. In either event, the hip's plumb cut is compound, with a 22½° bevel for a 45° bay.

Once the ledgers are installed, I plumb up from the lookouts below to locate any jack rafters. The jacks can then be measured directly. They have the same seat and plumb cut as the commons, except that the plumb cut is made with a 45° bevel.

Laying out the sheathing cuts is a matter of transferring measurements from the rafters. I usually add overhang to the sheathing to pick up the top edge of a crown molding.

Scott McBride is a contributing editor to Fine Homebuilding and the author of Build Like a Pro™: Windows and Doors, published by The Taunton Press.

Framing an Elegant Dormer

■ BY JOHN SPIER

Some years ago, my wife, Kerri, and I built a small Cape-style house for ourselves on Block Island, Rhode Island, where we live and work. Most small Capes have essentially the same upstairs plan: a central stairwell and a bathroom at the head of the stairs with bedrooms on each side. Dormers provide the headroom to make these upstairs spaces usable.

The most common arrangement is probably a doghouse, or gable, dormer in each of the bedrooms, with a larger dormer on the other side for the bathroom. Another alternative is a shed dormer over all three spaces, but we weren't too keen on that look. Then at some point, one of us found a picture of a dormer that was essentially two doghouse dormers connected by a shed dormer.

This design would give us as much interior space as a shed dormer, and it was a lot nicer looking. Of course, we argued over the choice at great length. Kerri, the artist, insisted on the beauty and complication of this hybrid dormer (photo, p. 106), while I, the practical carpenter, thought about how much easier and faster a basic shed dormer would be. I never had a chance of winning that argument.

As our dormer took shape, an old-timer on the island told us that what we were building was called a Nantucket dormer. The name stuck, and we use it to describe the several different variations that we've built since, including the project in this article. Ironically, the history experts on Nantucket island disavow any connection to the name, claiming that the design has no historical precedent.

Two Different Strategies for Two Different Interiors

Even though its design seems to be two dormers connected by a third, the Nantucket dormer is actually built as a single structure. The front wall can be a single plane, or its center section can be recessed. The project in this article has the center section stepped back, a look that I've come to prefer. As with most dormers, I think Nantucket dormers look better if the walls are set back from the

The doghouse-dormer wall is plumbed and braced in place.

Hybrid dormer. Doghouse dormers create more room and larger egress for the bedrooms at the ends of this house, while the shed room in between creates a space for a full bath.

The key element in supporting a Nantucket-dormer design is that it is point-loaded, either at the bases of the valleys or at the bottoms of the carrying rafters.

ends and edges of the main roof and from the plane of the walls below.

I frame Nantucket dormers two different ways to produce two distinctively different interiors. The difference, roughly speaking, is that one method uses structural rafters and the other uses structural valleys.

Framing the dormers with structural valleys allows the interior partitions to be eliminated, creating one big open room with interesting angular ceiling planes. For the project in this article, however, we used the structural-rafter method to create the more common floor plan with two bedrooms and a bath.

The key element in supporting a Nantucket-dormer design is that it is point-loaded, either at the bases of the valleys or at the bottoms of the carrying rafters. Those loads need to be carried by appropriate floor or wall structures below. The same frame that supports the uniform load of a shed dormer might not carry the point loads of a Nantucket dormer. If you have any doubts at all, it's a good idea to have a structural engineer evaluate the support structure.

Doghouse Walls Go Up First

After the main gables of the house are raised and braced, we lay out the locations of the main roof rafters on the top of the main wall plates. We also locate and snap lines for the outside walls of the doghouses and the shed on the second-floor deck.

The first things that we build are the two doghouse gables. We use the same process that we used for building and raising the main gables, only in a smaller scale. Just as with the main gables, the walls are framed, sheathed, housewrapped, and trimmed before they are lifted and braced plumb (photo, p. 105).

Next, we turn our attention to the main ridge of the house. Temporary scaffolding or pipe staging is set up down the middle of the house to work from while the ridge is set. We place the ridge boards (in this case, 2x12s) on top of the plates and transfer the rafter layout directly from plate to ridge (photo, below).

The ridge boards are set in their pockets and held up with temporary posts and a few common rafters, which help to keep them straight and level.

Laying out the ridge. To get the rafter layout to match precisely, the layout on the plates is transferred directly to the ridge stock.

Structural Rafters and Headers Form the Backbone of the Dormer Roof

With the ridge in place, the structural rafters adjacent to the doghouse walls are installed. We doubled these rafters using ½-in. plywood spacers in between to create a total thickness of 3½ in., which matches the width of wall plates for interior partitions below the doubled rafters. If you're building larger dormers, a triple rafter or a double LVL can be used.

The four sets of structural rafters split the main roof into three bays. Our next step is to hang doubled 2x12 headers in each of these bays. The tops of the headers are beveled to match the pitch of the rafters they hang from, and steel hangers hold the headers in place.

The two outside headers carry the valley rafters and the ridges of the doghouses. The

Backbone of an Elegant Dormer

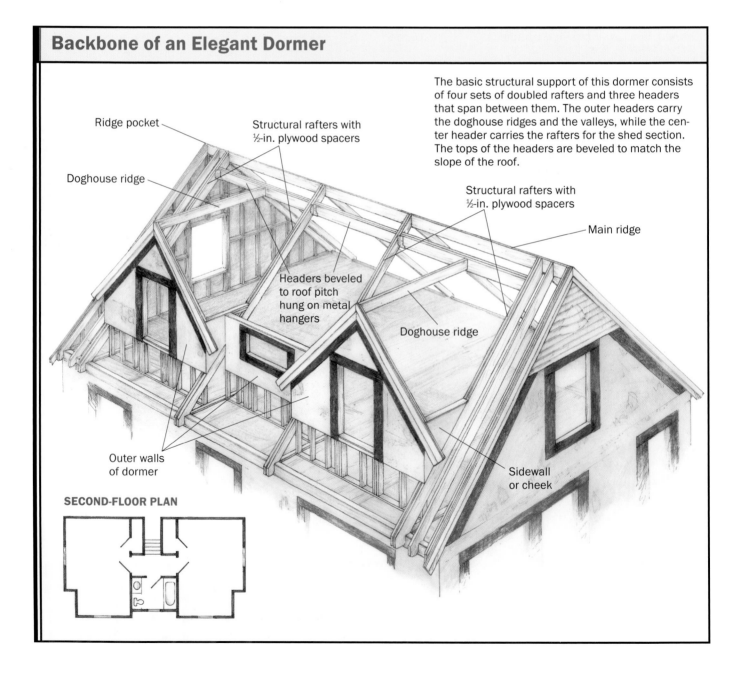

The basic structural support of this dormer consists of four sets of doubled rafters and three headers that span between them. The outer headers carry the doghouse ridges and the valleys, while the center header carries the rafters for the shed section. The tops of the headers are beveled to match the slope of the roof.

Ridge pocket

Structural rafters with ½-in. plywood spacers

Doghouse ridge

Structural rafters with ½-in. plywood spacers

Main ridge

Headers beveled to roof pitch hung on metal hangers

Doghouse ridge

Outer walls of dormer

Sidewall or cheek

SECOND-FLOOR PLAN

Doghouse ridge drops in. The doghouse ridge connects the outer wall of the doghouse dormer to the header.

center header holds the rafters of the shed section. Along with the structural rafters and the dormer walls, these headers form the backbone support for the dormer-roof structure (drawing, facing page).

While the headers are being built and installed, other crew members build and raise the front wall of the shed section. Next, we build and sheathe the triangular sidewalls, or cheeks, on the doghouses that support the common rafters for the two end sections. The doghouse ridges are dropped in next (photo, above), and their common rafters are cut and installed.

Lining up the Roof Planes and Soffits

Until this point, all the framing has been fairly routine. But now we bump into the chief complication in framing the Nantucket dormer, the fact that the shed roof in the middle is at a different pitch from the gable roofs of the doghouse dormers on each side. In this case, the pitch of the main house roof and the doghouse roofs was 12-in-12, and the shed roof worked out to be 7-in-12.

Different roof pitches mean that the valleys where the roof pitches intersect are irregular (they don't run at a 45° angle in plan). It also means that the roof planes have to align and that the rafter tails have to

Working Out the Details of the Shed Rafters

The rafters on the doghouse sections are 12-in-12 pitch, and the shed rafters are 7-in-12 pitch. A three-step drawing gets the fascias and soffits to line up, along with the roof and ceiling planes.

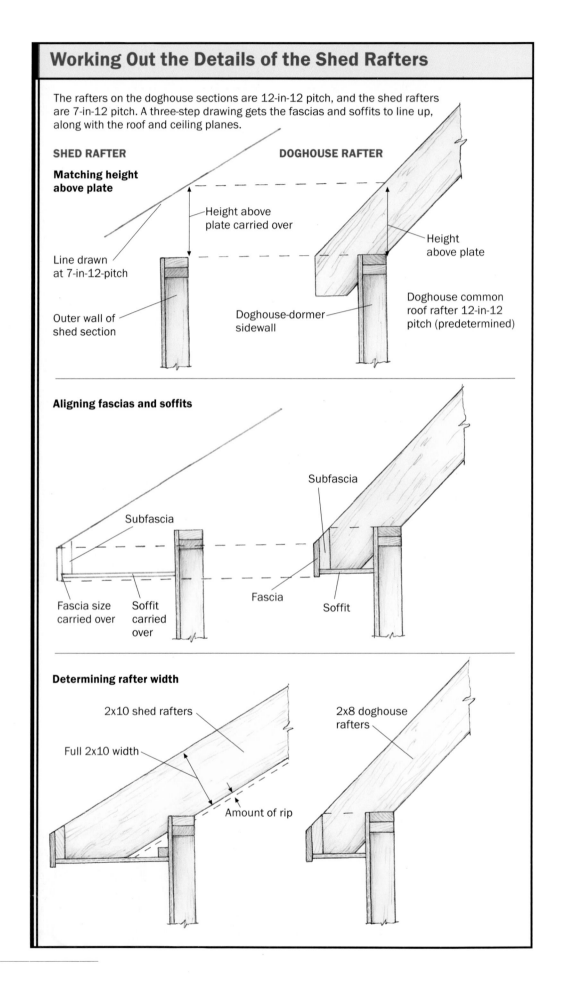

SHED RAFTER

DOGHOUSE RAFTER

Matching height above plate

Height above plate carried over

Line drawn at 7-in-12-pitch

Height above plate

Outer wall of shed section

Doghouse-dormer sidewall

Doghouse common roof rafter 12-in-12 pitch (predetermined)

Aligning fascias and soffits

Subfascia

Subfascia

Fascia

Fascia size carried over

Soffit carried over

Soffit

Determining rafter width

2x10 shed rafters

2x8 doghouse rafters

Full 2x10 width

Amount of rip

be adjusted to get consistent fascia heights and soffit levels. So early on in the process, I work out the rafter details (drawings, facing page). These elements can be worked out on the drawing board, but most often, I make a full-scale drawing of the trim details on either rafter stock or on a sheet of plywood. With this on-site drawing, I can design the rafter tails before I pick up a saw.

Another complication caused by the differing roof pitches is getting the planes of the cathedral ceiling inside to line up. Obviously, a 2x10 rafter meeting a valley at a 12-in-12 pitch will do so at a much different depth than one meeting it at a 7-in-12 pitch. The simplest approach to this problem is to increase the size of the framing material for the shed-roof section. With dormer gables at the same pitch as the main roof, the vertical depth of the rafters at the plate can be measured. The central shed portion of the dormer has a shallower pitch, so it requires a larger rafter size to achieve the same vertical dimension. For this project, the doghouse rafters were made of 2x8s, but the shed-roof rafters had to be 2x10s. But for the roof planes outside and the ceiling planes inside to match up, the 2x10s had to be ripped down to around 9 in. (sidebar, right).

Valleys Are Strung and Measured

Four years of architecture and engineering school taught me that it is possible to work out the framing details of an irregular valley using math and geometry. They even gave me the tools and education to do it. But 20 years as a carpenter have taught me that figuring out irregular valleys is faster and easier with a taut string.

After cutting and installing the common rafters and subfascia for both the doghouses and shed, I stretch a string from the corner where the subfascias meet up to the intersection of the header and the doghouse ridge. From this string, I measure the length of the valley rafters (top photo, facing page) as well

Finding the Exact Rip

Once the stock size of the shed rafters has been determined (in this case, 2x10), a simple procedure determines the final rafter width. First, the height-above-plate distance is measured for the 2x8 doghouse-dormer rafters. Next, that distance is transferred to a plumb-cut line at the shed-rafter pitch. That point marks the final width of the rafter.

Height above plate for doghouse rafter at 12-in-12 pitch

Height above plate at 7-in-12 pitch plumb cut

Full width of 2x8

Remove this amount.

Final rafter width

Full width of 2x10

Measuring an irregular valley. The quickest way to figure out the irregular valley is to stretch a line from corner to corner. Here, a measurement is taken along that line.

Finding the plumb cut. A rafter square held in the corner against the string determines the angle of the valley plumb cuts.

Corner of the valley. Angles that are taken on each side of the string determine the corner cuts that are needed for the ends of the valley rafter.

Valley rafter slips into place. After all the angles have been cut into the valley rafters, including a bevel on the bottom edge where the ceiling planes intersect, the valleys are nailed in permanently.

as the angles of the top and bottom plumb cuts (bottom left photo, facing page), the seat-cut angle and the bevel angles I need to cut into the rafter ends (bottom right photo, facing page). Armed with all this information, I cut a valley rafter and drop it into place. Then, using a straightedge from the commons on each side, I mark the bevel cuts on the bottom edge.

After cutting the bevels, I install the valley rafters permanently (photo, above) and then lay out and measure the jack rafters. The jack rafters in the center section usually have a compound cut where the miter is beyond the 45° or even 60° that most saws can cut.

If I have a lot of those cuts to make or if the framing is going to be left exposed, I make my cuts with a jig using either a handsaw or a reciprocating saw to make a clean, accurate cut. However, the typical dormer has only three or four jack rafters per side, so I mark the angles on the rafter stock and cut them with a circular saw as close as the saw allows. I carve out the remainder of the wood by slowly and carefully dragging the circular saw blade across the face of the cut. This operation is potentially dangerous, so if you're not comfortable with it, you can use one of the methods mentioned above.

Jack rafters complete the framing. With the valleys in place, jacks are cut and installed to finish the framing of the roof planes.

The Rest is Plywood

While jacks are being cut and fit (photo, above), other crew members fill in the cripple rafters that complete the main roof framing below the three dormer sections. The subfascia is applied to the main eaves, and we can start running the sheathing. Other than the fact that the various plywood shapes are somewhat irregular, sheathing proceeds in the usual fashion, working from the eaves up.

With the outside framed, sheathed, and ready for roofing, we can turn our attention to the inside. The interior of a Nantucket dormer is usually finished with a cathedral ceiling, which helps the small second-story spaces to feel more spacious and airy.

Instead of applying the cathedral-ceiling finishes directly to the bottoms of the rafters, here in New England, we nail 1x3 strapping to the rafters, usually 12 in. or 16 in. o.c.

Strapping the ceilings of the Nantucket dormer not only simplifies board hanging, providing an extra measure of resistance to deflection and nail popping, but the strapping also helps to provide a smooth, easy transition between the various ceiling planes. To this end, I usually supplement the strapping by running 1x6 or 1x4 on the undersides of the valley rafters where the roof planes intersect.

John Spier and his wife, Kerri, have a general-contracting and renovation business on Block Island, Rhode Island.

Skinning the dormer. When the framing is complete, the sheathing is applied, bringing out the final dramatic shape of the Nantucket dormer.

A Gable-Dormer Retrofit

■ BY SCOTT McBRIDE

Carol and Scott Little's home draws its inspiration from the cottages of colonial Williamsburg and the one-and-a-half story homes of Cape Cod. Both styles typically feature a pair of front-facing gable dormers. But for some reason, the builder of the Littles's house put only one dormer on the front, leaving the facade looking unbalanced. I was hired to add a new dormer on the front of the house to match the existing one and, for more light, added a scaled-down version of the same dormer on the back of the single-story wing.

As the crew set up the scaffolding and rigged the tarps against the possibility of rain (sidebar, p. 118), I crawled under the eaves to study the existing roof. I soon realized that framing the sidewalls of the two dormers and directing their load paths would require different strategies, as would the way the dormer ridges would be tied to the main roof.

The first consideration in a retrofit is the location of the dormers, and the second is their framing. The existing front dormer fit neatly into three bays of the 16-in. o. c. main-roof rafters. These main-roof rafters (or commons) were doubled up on each side of the dormer, creating the trimmer rafters that carry the roof load for the dormers. Full-height dormer sidewalls stood just inside these trimmers, extending into the house as far as the bedroom kneewalls. Additional in-fill framing completed the dormer walls that were above the sloped bedroom ceiling.

Fortunately, three rafter bays at the other end of the roof landed within a few inches of balancing with the location of the existing dormer. Consequently, I had only to sister new rafters to the insides of the existing ones to form the new trimmers, and I could match the framing of the existing front dormer, leaving a uniform roof placement, appearance and size.

Cut the Opening and Shore Up the Main-Roof Framing First

After laying out the plan of the front dormer on the subfloor, I used a plumb bob to project its two front corners up to the underside of the roof sheathing. Drilling through the roof at this location established the reference points for removing the shingles and cutting the openings.

The tricky part was establishing how far up the slope to cut the opening. To play it

Protecting the Roof

To protect the exposed roof against rain, we rolled up new poly tarps around 2x4s and mounted them on the roof ridge above each dormer. The tarps were rolled down like window shades each evening, with some additional lumber laid on top as ballast. The ballast boards were tacked together as a crude framework so that they would not blow away individually in high winds.

safe, I first opened just enough room to raise the full-height portion of the sidewalls (drawing, p. 120). With those walls up and later with some dormer rafters in place, I could project back to the roof to define the valley and then enlarge the opening accordingly.

Inserting new rafters into an already-sheathed roof can be problematic because of the shape of the rafters. They are much longer along the top edge than along the bottom, so there's no way to slip them up from below. A standard 16-in. bay doesn't afford nearly enough room to angle them in, either. To form the new trimmer rafters, we cut the new members about 6 in. short of the wall plate before we secured them to the existing rafters.

When faced with this situation, I normally use posts to transfer the load from the trimmer rafters to an above-floor header. In fact, I did follow this step with the smaller rear dormer (sidebar, pp. 122-123), but that would not work in this case. Here, the floor joists ran parallel to the front wall, instead of perpendicular to it, and so could not transfer the load to the wall.

I decided simply to let the existing single rafter carry the load for the last 6 in. to the front wall plate. This situation is not the ideal solution, but the weight of the dormer is not great enough to overtax the rafters over such a short span, and doubling up the new trimmer rafters would at least stiffen the existing rafters considerably.

With the new trimmer rafters in, the existing main-roof rafters falling between them were cut and partially torn out to make room for the dormers. The portions above and below the dormer would remain as cripple rafters. The lower cripple rafters were plumb-cut in line with the dormer front wall where they would be spiked to cripple studs. Rough cuts were then made at the top, leaving the upper cripple rafters long. These rafters would be trimmed back further only later, after we established the precise location of the dormer-roof header.

To support the upper cripple rafters temporarily, I climbed up into the little attic above the bedroom. There I laid a 2x4 strongback across four collar ties, including the collar ties connected to the recently doubled trimmers. This strongback would support both the collar ties and the upper cripple rafters until we could install the dormer-roof header.

Dormer Sidewalls Can be Framed Two Ways

With trimmer rafters installed and cripple rafters secured, I could proceed with the walls. I know two common ways to frame dormer sidewalls: You can stand a full-height wall next to a trimmer rafter, or you can build a triangular sidewall on top of a trimmer rafter, which is how I framed the rear dormer. To match the new front dormer to the existing one, I used full-height studs 16 in. o. c. only as far in as the kneewall.

This type of dormer sidewall normally delivers the weight of a dormer to the floor. In new construction, this weight is taken up by doubling the floor joists under these walls. I didn't want to tear out the finished floor, however, so I joined the full-length sidewalls to the trimmer rafters by predrilling and pounding two 6-in. barn spikes through each stud. This transferred the load to the trimmer rafters rather than placing it on the floor framing. I've seen barn spikes withstand tremendous shear loads in agricultural buildings, so I felt confident they could carry this little dormer.

Plan the Cornice Details Before Framing the Roof

With the walls up, the roof framing, which is the most complicated, came next. Before cutting any dormer rafters, though, I drew a full-scale cornice section, using the existing dormer as a model. Worrying about

Supporting the Dormer

After doubling the rafters flanking each dormer, the author cut out the existing rafters where they crossed through the dormer. He installed a strongback across the collar ties to support the upper cripple rafters until the roof header was in place. Because the floor joists ran parallel to the front wall instead of sitting on it, the author transferred the weight from the sidewalls to the trimmer rafters with 6-in. spikes.

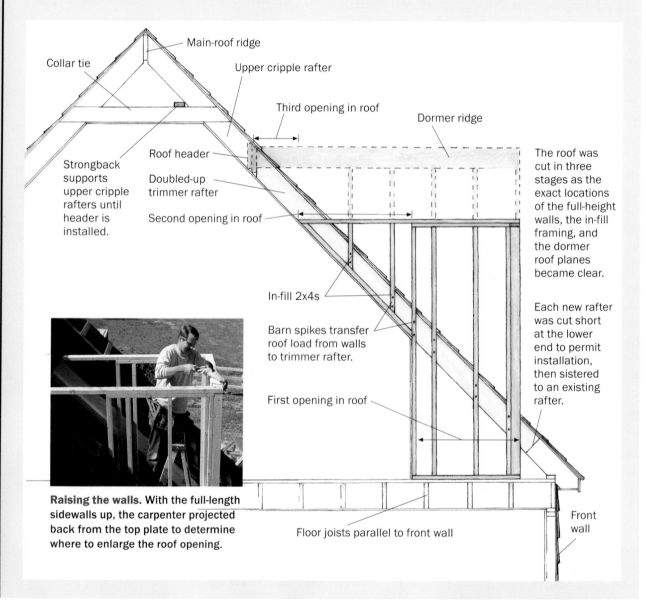

Main-roof ridge

Collar tie

Upper cripple rafter

Third opening in roof

Dormer ridge

Roof header

Strongback supports upper cripple rafters until header is installed.

Doubled-up trimmer rafter

Second opening in roof

The roof was cut in three stages as the exact locations of the full-height walls, the in-fill framing, and the dormer roof planes became clear.

In-fill 2x4s

Barn spikes transfer roof load from walls to trimmer rafter.

Each new rafter was cut short at the lower end to permit installation, then sistered to an existing rafter.

First opening in roof

Raising the walls. With the full-length sidewalls up, the carpenter projected back from the top plate to determine where to enlarge the roof opening.

Floor joists parallel to front wall

Front wall

trim before there is even a roof may seem like the tail wagging the dog; but it makes sense, especially in a retrofit. The existing dormer featured a pediment above the window. The eaves had neither soffit nor fascia, just a crown molding making the transition from the frieze board to the roof (photo, facing page). That detail reduced the dormer rafter tail to a mere horn that would catch the top of the crown molding. The eaves section drawing helped to establish the cuts for the rafter tails and trim details.

Along the rakes, the crown molding was picked up by the roof sheathing, which was

A crowning moment. Three pieces of crown converge at the bottom corners of the pediment. Trim, casings, and sills, primed on every side, resist rot.

beveled and extended out past the gable wall. Using a short piece of molding as a template, I worked out the amount of the overhang and the correct bevel for the edge of the sheathing in the rake-section drawing. Juxtaposing the drawings ensured that the rake crown, the eave crown and the level-return crown would all converge crisply at a single point.

Framing the Roof Defines the Valleys

Ready to proceed with the roof framing, we set up two pairs of common rafters with a temporary ridge board between them. Then we used a straightedge to project the outline of the dormer roof planes onto the main roof and cut back the main-roof sheathing accordingly (drawing, p. 124). Having established the elevation of the dormer ridge, we

Unfortunately, when it came to the smaller dormer in back, the existing rafter layout did not match where the dormer needed to be, as was the case in front. Here, I had to build new trimmer rafters in the middle of the existing rafter bays.

The attic space differed, too. Whereas the front dormer served a bedroom, the back dormer was in a storage room.

Because the owner wanted to maximize floor space in this storage area, I built the sidewalls on top of the rafters, which pushed the kneewall back and allowed the ceiling slope to extend all the way to the dormer's gable wall (drawing, below).

As in the front dormer, we cut the new trimmer rafters short. This time, however, the floor joists ran perpendicular to the

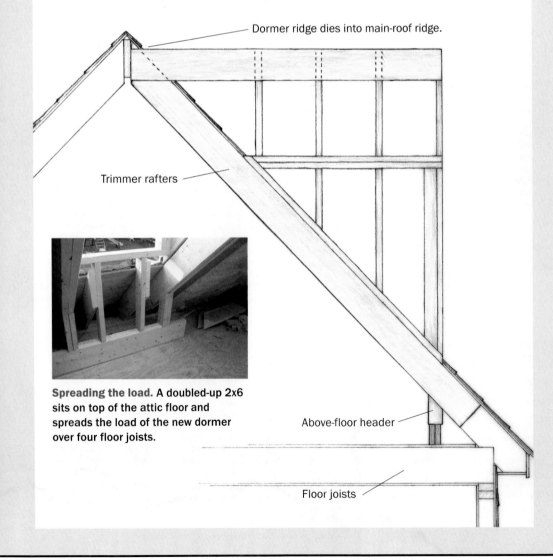

ABOVE-FLOOR HEADER DISTRIBUTES WEIGHT OF THE DORMER. There wasn't enough room in the existing roof structure to install full-length trimmer rafters that would bear on the exterior wall. Instead, the trimmers were cut short, and an above-floor header was used to transfer their loads to the floor joists and to the exterior wall.

Dormer ridge dies into main-roof ridge.

Trimmer rafters

Spreading the load. A doubled-up 2x6 sits on top of the attic floor and spreads the load of the new dormer over four floor joists.

Above-floor header

Floor joists

Because this dormer's roof ridge was at the same elevation as the main-roof ridge, I tied the dormer ridge and the main-roof ridge directly together instead of building a separate dormer header.

Measuring and cutting the valley rafters was the same for the back as for the front with the exception that at the bottom of the back dormer's valley rafters, the compound miters did not need a level seat cut because the valley rafters would not sit on top of 2x4 wall plates. Instead, the valley rafters were simply nailed to the face of the trimmer rafters.

In the doghouse. Narrow dormers are prone to racking. To stiffen this one, the author sheathed the front wall with a single sheet of plywood.

front and back walls, which meant that I could use posts to transfer the load from the trimmer rafters to an above-floor header (photo, facing page). The header distributes the weight over several floor joists, and the joists carry the weight back to the wall. The additional strain imposed on the floor joists is minimal because the header is so close to the wall.

The location of the back dormer's roof ridge altered another aspect of the framing.

Finding the bottom of the valley. A straightedge is laid across the dormer rafters to project the roof surface to the inside of the trimmer rafter.

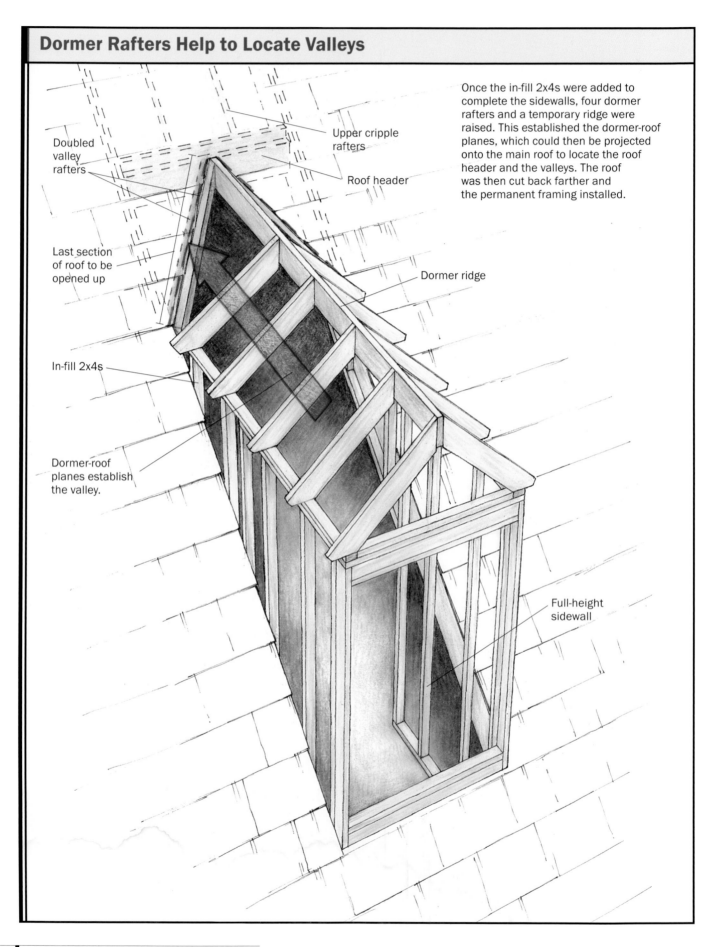

Doubled valley rafters

Upper cripple rafters

Roof header

Once the in-fill 2x4s were added to complete the sidewalls, four dormer rafters and a temporary ridge were raised. This established the dormer-roof planes, which could then be projected onto the main roof to locate the roof header and the valleys. The roof was then cut back farther and the permanent framing installed.

Last section of roof to be opened up

Dormer ridge

In-fill 2x4s

Dormer-roof planes establish the valley.

Full-height sidewall

trimmed back the upper cripple rafters and then installed the roof header to carry the permanent dormer ridge board. The roof header spans between the trimmer rafters, carrying the dormer ridge and the valley rafters. (On the rear dormer, the ridge was level with the main-roof ridge, so no header was necessary there.)

When the dormer common rafters and ridge were installed permanently, we used the straightedge again to find the intersection of the dormer roof planes and the inside face of each trimmer rafter (bottom photo, p. 123). This point is where the centers of the valley rafters would meet the trimmer rafters. At their tops, the valley rafters would nuzzle into the right angle formed between the dormer ridge and the main-roof header.

I like to "back" my valley rafters, a process of beveling them so that they accept the sheathing of each adjoining roof on its respective plane. Because a cathedral ceiling was to wrap under the valley, I backed the lower edge of the valley as well, giving a nice surface for attaching drywall.

In addition to backing, I double valleys, even when not structurally necessary, because it gives ample bearing for plywood above and drywall below. Doubling valley rafters also simplifies the cheek-cut layout at the top and bottom of the valley because a single compound miter is made on each piece instead of a double compound miter on a single piece.

Because of the dormer's diminutive size, valley jack rafters weren't required. Consequently, with the valleys in place, the framing was complete, and we could dry it in.

Careful Sheathing and Flashing Combat Wind and Water

We sheathed the front of each dormer with a single piece of plywood for maximum shear strength (top photo, p. 123). With so little wall area next to the windows, I was

concerned that the dormer might rack in high winds. The small back dormer was especially worrisome because it had no full-length sidewalls to combat racking, but the single piece of plywood on its front stiffened the whole structure. We extended the roof sheathing past the gable wall and beveled it to receive the rake crown molding.

Keep the water moving down. An apron flashing seals the front wall with its ends bent around the corners (top). Then the lowest step flashings have their vertical fins bent over to cover the notches in the apron (bottom).

Water-table flashing protects window and trim. The crown that forms the bottom of the pediment will go below the flashed water table and miter with an eaves crown (seen poking out past the corner).

Flashing work began with an aluminum apron flashing at the bottom of the dormer front wall (top photo, p. 125). The downhill fin of this flashing extends a few inches beyond both sides of the dormer, and its vertical fin was notched and folded back along the sidewall. Then the first piece of step flashing had its vertical fin folded back along the front wall to protect the corners where the apron flashing had been notched (bottom photo, p. 125). Step flashings march up along both sides of the dormer, with the uppermost pieces trimmed to fit tightly beneath the dormer roof sheathing. It was tough work weaving step flashings into the existing cedar-shake roof. Hidden nails had to be extracted with a shingle ripper, a tool with a flat, hooked blade. If I had it to do over, I would sever these nails with a reciprocating saw before the dormer sidewalls were framed.

The valley flashing was trimmed flush with the dormer ridge on one side of the roof, and the opposing valley flashing was notched so that it could be bent over the ridge. We protected the point where the valleys converge at the dormer ridge with a small flap of aluminum with its corners bent into the valley. This approach is more reliable than caulk.

The last piece of flashing to go on was the gable water-table flashing (photo, facing page). Its front edge turns down over the return crown molding, and its rear corners fold up under the extended roof sheathing to repel wind-driven rain.

Durable Finish Trim is Important

The house is just a few years old, but the existing front dormer had suffered extensive decay. In the worst shape were the finger-jointed casings and sill extensions that the original builder had used. To avoid a repeat of this calamity, I used only solid moldings and bought cedar for the trim boards. Everything was primed, especially the ends. To promote air circulation, the ends of corner boards and rake boards were elevated an inch or so above nearby flashings.

We wanted the new cedar shakes on the dormer to blend in with the existing weathered roof. I asked around for a stain recipe, but the only response I got was from an old farmer standing at the lumberyard counter. He insisted that horse manure was the ticket. To my great relief, we hit upon a more savory alternative. We brushed on an undercoat of Minwax® Jacobean, followed by a top coat of oil-based exterior stain in a driftwood-type shade. The undercoat added a nice depth to the gray top coat.

Scott McBride is a contributing editor of Fine Homebuilding and the author of Build Like a Pro™: Windows and Doors, published by The Taunton Press.

To promote air circulation, the ends of corner boards and rake boards were elevated an inch or so above nearby flashings.

Raising Roof Trusses

■ BY RICK ARNOLD AND MIKE GUERTIN

We learned truss raising the hard way. Fingers trapped between sliding trusses were broken, and backs were strained muscling 32-ft.-wide trusses up two stories for steep-pitched colonial roofs. The process involved six or seven guys and usually lasted a whole frustrating, tiring day. The process was tough on the trusses as well. Lifting them flat would cause the truss plates to bend or pop, ruining the truss. If we were lucky enough to get all of the trusses installed in a day, we then faced the arduous task of lugging up all of the sheathing and roofing materials. After all of that hauling and lifting, there wasn't much enthusiasm or energy for swinging a hammer. Our lives got much simpler after we opened the phone book to the listing for "Cranes."

We have come to depend on a crane to lift the trusses for all but the smallest single-story roofs. In this article we'll discuss how we use a crane to assemble simple gable roofs.

Before the roofing materials and trusses are dropped at the site, we anticipate where the crane will be positioned so that all materials are out of the way but still easily within reach. Before the trusses are lifted to the roof, the crane hoists the sheathing, the shingles, and the interior-framing materials for the second floor (sidebar, pp. 134-135). The crane we hire can usually reach an entire house and garage from one position near the outside middle of the building. We also keep the job site as clean as possible. Scrap lumber and debris can be accidents waiting to happen on raising day. Our scrap pile is always located out of the way but still within tossing distance of the house.

When the trusses arrive, we land them on top of 2x blocks as they come off the truck to keep them as flat and as much out of the dirt as possible. Sometimes trusses arrive as much as a week before they can be installed. If the trusses are not kept flat, they can warp, and after they've warped, they're much harder to install.

Instant, ready-made gable. With the sheathing, shingles, and trim boards already attached, the only thing this gable needs is the vent. The crew will leave the peak of this gable just tacked in place until the overall length of the house is checked at the eaves and the peak.

Stacked for easy layout. With the trusses stacked neatly on the ground, layout lines are drawn on all of them at once. The line closest to the tail will be used to position the truss on top of the wall plates. The other lines are for ceiling strapping. The top chords are laid out for roof sheathing.

Layouts Are Done with the Trusses on the Ground

We mark three different sets of layout lines on the trusses before they ever get off the ground. The first set is for positioning the trusses on the walls. The second is for the strapping or furring strips to which we'll screw the drywall or plasterboard ceilings, and the last set of lines is for the roof sheathing.

We also mark the front of the trusses near the tail of the top chord to avoid getting them spun in reverse when they're lifted. Before we mark these lines, the trusses need to be aligned on top of one another as closely as possible. We arrange them in a stack by tapping them back and forth with a sledgehammer until all of the bottom chords and ridges are in line. When the trusses are in a straight stack, we can make our layout lines.

In the past we aligned the trusses after they were raised. We would run a string from one gable peak to the other and bang the trusses back and forth with a sledgehammer until they lined up with the string. But all of that banging knocked the walls out of plumb, and the whole process took a lot of time. We also tried measuring in from the tail cuts to position the trusses but soon discovered that those distances varied significantly and that the peaks of the trusses didn't line up. Now we mark the wall position on the bottom chord of the trusses before we lift them; it's the quickest, most accurate way of ensuring that the trusses are installed in a straight line.

First we measure the overall width of the house where the trusses will sit. Then we locate the exact center of the bottom chord on the top truss of our pile and measure back half of the width of the building minus the thickness of the wall from that point. For example, if the house is 30 ft. wide with 2x4 walls, we would measure back 14 ft. 8⅜ in. from the center point (figuring the walls at 3⅝ in.). We mark each end of the top truss and then repeat the whole process on the lowest truss in the pile. We either snap a chalkline or scribe a line along a straightedge between the top and bottom marks to transfer the layout to the other trusses. We extend our position lines slightly onto the face of the bottom chord to make it easier to see the lines when the trusses are being dropped into place.

Ceilings in our region are typically strapped with 1x3 furring strips before the interior walls and wallboard are installed. Furring strips serve several functions, one of which is adding a structural element to the trusses. If we didn't use strapping, the truss engineer would require us to run three or four 2x braces the length of the building to tie the trusses together and also to keep the gable walls straight.

We mark the lines for the furring strips 16 in. o. c. from the positioning marks at one end of the truss. Again, the same marks are made on the top and bottom trusses, and lines are drawn or snapped between them. We run a lumber crayon up one side of each line to indicate which side of the line our furring gets nailed to once the trusses are set.

The last set of layout lines is for the roof sheathing. We usually fill in any ripped sheets at the bottom of the roof rather than at the top, so we begin our layout from the ridge. First we measure down along the top chord of the upper truss from the peak to the 4-ft. increment nearest the tail of the truss. We add ⅛ in. per sheet for the H-clips plus an extra ¼ in. to our overall measurement to be safe. For example, if the top chord of the truss is 17 ft. 6 in., we would measure 16 ft. ¾ in. (4 sheets x ⅛ in. = ½ in.; ½ in. + ¼ in. = ¾ in.) If a ridge vent is being installed, we increase our extra amount to a full 1 in., and our layout line is at 16 ft. ½ in. The top chords of the lowest truss in the pile are marked at the same points, and lines are drawn or snapped between the marks.

Getting the Signals Straight

Communication between the crane operator and crew is essential for safe and smooth lifting. A designated signal person has the responsibility of directing the lifting operation through hand signals. Here are the four basic hand signals we use with all of our crane operators.

Cable up/cable down

To move a load straight up or down, the crane operator must take up or let out the cable holding the load. To signal this procedure to the operator, point one finger either straight up or straight down and spin your hand in a circle.

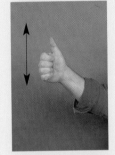

Boom up/boom down

Raising the boom on the crane moves the load toward the crane, and lowering the boom sends the load away. The signal for this procedure is a thumb pointed either up or down with the hand moving in an up or down motion.

Boom right/boom left

Moving a load side to side is accomplished by pivoting the crane and boom. Pointing a finger to one side or the other in the direction you want the load to move is the proper signal for this procedure.

Stop and hold

To hold a load still momentarily, for example, while positioning blocks on the deck for materials to land on, a fist held stationary in the air stops the crane operation until the next signal is given.

A big time-saver is sheathing, siding, and trimming the gable-end trusses while they are still on the ground.

Nails for attaching the gable truss are started on the ground. To facilitate setting the gable truss, nails are started along the bottom chord. When the truss is in position, a crew member on a ladder will drive the nails into the top plate of the gable-end wall.

Gable Trusses Are Sheathed and Sided before They Go Up

Another big time-saver that we've found is sheathing, siding, and trimming the gable-end trusses while they are still on the ground (photo, facing page). It saves us the hassle of setting up tall staging to work up high and requires just a little planning. Because the gable trusses sit on top of walls, we make sure that there are no humps in the wall or dips in the bottom chord of the truss. We check the walls by eye and string the bottom chord of the gable trusses. If necessary, we rip a little off the bottom of the bottom chord of the truss.

We always plan to extend our gable-truss sheathing down beyond the bottom chord of the truss a couple of inches. To set this overhang, we run a string between the seat positions of the truss and measure from the string to set our sheathing. We always leave the sheathing ¼ in. short to avoid any binding between the gable-wall sheathing and the truss sheathing when we're setting the truss. The gable truss must be lying absolutely flat when the sheathing is applied, or it may be impossible to straighten the truss when it's installed. Any sheathing that extends above the top chord gets trimmed off flush.

If no rake overhangs are called for, siding the gable goes quickly. We start by figuring out the approximate height of the top of the second-floor windows (they don't get installed until after the trusses) and determine the siding courses from there. It's best to start one or two courses up from the bottom of the truss sheathing so that the siding doesn't interfere with the truss installation. Wood siding allows us to adjust our course exposure slightly to blend the siding on the walls with the truss siding. We've never tried this technique with vinyl siding and suspect that it would be difficult to match the courses exactly. We're careful to nail the bottom course of the truss siding

up high so that the course coming up from below can be slipped in later.

With no rake overhangs, we run the siding over the top chord of the truss but keep the nails 3 in. back from the top of the chord. The gable-vent hole can be cut out at this point, and the vent tacked in for installing the siding. The vent is then removed to give us a hole for our lifting straps, and it is reinstalled later (photo, p. 129). When there are no gable vents, we leave off the last couple of siding courses at the top of the truss and cut a hole for the straps. We precut the missing siding pieces and tack them to the gable end to be nailed on later from a ladder.

After the siding is nailed on, we snap a chalkline 2½ in. down from the top edge of the top chord and cut the siding off to that line. We nail on a piece of 1x3 above the cut siding as a spacer. The rake boards and band moldings are nailed over the 1x3, and the height of the rake boards is adjusted to match the thickness of the roof sheathing. We leave the tails of the rake boards long and cut them off after the gable truss is set in place.

If rake overhangs are called for, we take extra care to keep the top chord of the truss perfectly straight while we're sheathing the truss. We make our overhangs out of a 2x4 ladder with waste sheathing nailed to the top side of it to keep it stable. The overhang assembly is nailed to the sheathed gable truss, keeping the top of the assembly flush with the top of the truss. We install ½-in. AC plywood on the underside of the overhangs for our soffits and nail the rake boards and band moldings to the outside of the ladder, again adjusting for the thickness of the roof sheathing. We side the gable the same as before except that now the siding butts to the plywood soffit and a 1x2 frieze board is added.

Let a Crane Do the Heavy Lifting

No matter what your physical condition, reducing the amount of bull work on the job is always welcome. A crane is one great way of saving muscles as well as man-hours and money (our crane operator usually charges around $65 per hour). Before the trusses are raised, the crane lifts the roof sheathing, second-floor interior-wall studs, furring strips, and roof shingles to the second floor.

Materials Are Prepped for Lifting ahead of Time

With a rough count of all of the second-floor interior studs we'll need, we crown, cut, and stack all of the framing stock on 3-ft. to 4-ft. scraps of 2x4 (photo, below).

The roof shingles are usually delivered the day before the truss raising, along with several extra pallets to stack them on. We generally stack 21 to 24 bundles per pallet and use a long hook that the crane operator made to feed the lifting strap through the pallet. We use 3-ft. 2x4s as strap spreaders to keep the lifting straps from crunching the top bundles of shingles (top photo, facing page). Roofing subcontractors love having the shingles on the second floor. Passing the bundles out a window, onto the staging and up to the roof is much easier and safer than hauling them up two stories on a ladder.

The roof sheathing is sent out at the same time as the shingles. Our lumberyard

Interior wall framing on the rise. Lumber is stacked ahead of time for an easy crane hoist; crew members land the framing lumber inside the house where it will be out of the way until it's needed.

will band sheets of plywood in any quantity that we ask. Bundles of 15 to 20 sheets for ⅝-in. plywood or bundles of 20 to 25 sheets for ½-in. plywood seem to work best for us (bottom photo). When the sheathing is slid off the delivery truck, we ask the driver to put heavy-duty nylon load straps around the entire stack to keep the steel bands from snapping. Occasionally, we get lucky and are able to coordinate delivery of the sheathing and shingles with the actual lift. In those rare instances the crane plucks the sheathing and shingles right off the delivery truck and lifts them up to the second floor.

Placement of the Materials on the Second-Floor Deck Takes a Bit of Planning

Roof sheathing and the furring will be used up before the interior walls are built so that material can go almost anywhere. The studs and the roof shingles, however, need to be positioned so that they won't interfere with framing the interior walls. We try to land the stacks near windows for easy handling, and because of the concentrated weight, we keep them away from the middle of the floor joists to avoid overloading them.

When rigging the bundles and stacks with the lifting straps, we try to keep the straps as far apart on the load as possible. The crane operator takes the strain slowly so that we can make sure the load is going to stay flat and even while it's in the air. It's not uncommon to have a load put back down on the ground to get the straps positioned just right. This minor hassle is infinitely preferable to a load coming apart or straps shifting and sliding while a load is in midair.

Roof shingles are dropped near a window. The crew member on the left signals the crane operator while the other crew member guides the pallet of shingles to its temporary home.

Prepackaged loads of sheathing are easier to handle. The lumber company bundles the sheathing in stacks of 15 to 20 sheets for easy strapping and lifting.

We often have a chimney or chimney chase on the gable ends of our houses. Before siding the truss, we meet with the mason and determine the location of the chimney so that we can break back the siding and rake trim to his dimensions. After the gable truss is installed, we drop a plumb bob from the gable siding to the fireplace footing and snap a chalkline for the mason to go by. The final step in prepping the gable truss is starting nails in the bottom of the truss that will attach the bottom chord of the truss to the end-wall plate (photo, p. 132).

Using a Nailer Saves a Truss

After the trusses are ready, there are other preparations that make the raising go more smoothly. First we set up all of the staging front and rear. All of the walls that will receive the trusses are laid out, and strings are set up along the inside of the top plates for straightening the walls. We install adjustable diagonal braces to help straighten and tune the walls. We double-check the plans to see where the second-floor walls will be built in order to locate the best out-of-the-way places to drop materials (sidebar, pp. 134-135). We build a lot of two-story colonials with single-story attached garages. We save the cost of one truss by using a nailer in place of the truss that ordinarily would go against the wall of house (photo, left). We slide one truss up before the crane arrives and use it as a template to mark the nailer location. After installing the nailer on the house wall, we set the truss in place and wait for the crane do the rest.

We also lay out ten 16-ft. pieces of 1x3 with 2-ft. centers for truss spacing and have another ten ready for diagonal bracing. We round up a bunch of clubs, 3-ft. to 4-ft. pieces of 2x4, to put under and between the piles of materials when the crane drops them off on the second floor.

The first gable truss is sent up with two regular trusses. By sending the first three trusses up together, the crane will be able to hold the gable truss steady while the other trusses are set and while braces are attached to the gable truss.

Crew Members Have Assigned Tasks for the Lift

As truss-raising day approaches, we watch the weather carefully. The best weather for raising trusses is calm and overcast. Wind is our worst enemy, and bright sun can make it difficult to see hand signals as well as trusses in midair. We always shoot for an early start when the sun's angle is low and when the winds are usually calmest. Before the actual lifting begins, we round up all of the tools we'll need for the raising, including the truss spacers, a level, and a straightedge for plumbing the first gable, and braces for holding and adjusting the first gable-end truss. We also get the tag line ready, fill our pouches with nails and recheck the walls to make sure they are straight. We also set up a ladder on the end of the house to make it easier to nail the bottom of the gable truss.

We always prefer to be a little overstaffed on raising day. Everyone has assigned duties, and the most important task is signaling the crane operator. We have used the same operator for six years, and we try to have the same crew member do the signaling for every raising (sidebar, p. 131). For safety's sake we always review the hand signals with the crane operator and the crew member who will be signaling. A thumb pointed in the wrong direction could get someone knocked off the staging in an instant. The signal person should never leave the crane operator's sight unless he signals "stop and hold."

For lifting materials, two crew members on the ground strap and launch loads, and two or three other crew members inside the house land and unstrap loads. The signal person usually sits in a second-floor window where he can watch materials coming in and see the crane operator clearly. After materials are secured on the second floor, we reposition the crew for the trusses.

The signal person is now stationed on the staging at the front of the house to set truss ends and to signal the crane operator. A second crew member is on the rear staging to orient the positioning marks on the trusses to the inside of the wall and to nail the trusses to the rear-wall plates. Two other crew members work in the middle of the trusses, tying them together at the peak when the crane drops them in. A crew member on the ground puts the trusses on the hook or strap and handles the tag line that steadies the trusses en route from the ground to the house. A sixth person is useful but not absolutely necessary to act as a gofer and to help when needed.

Lifting the First Three Trusses at Once Is Safe and Easy

Setting the first gable truss can be tricky. The best way we've found is sending that truss aloft with two other trusses, but with the gable truss in a separate strap (photo, facing page). If we sent up the gable truss by itself, we would have to depend on a brace with a steep angle to hold the gable until other trusses could be set. Our method lets the crane hold the gable truss steady until two other trusses are set and safer braces can be attached. Here's how it works.

After landing the first three trusses at the end of the house, the bottoms of the two regular trusses are kicked away from the gable about a foot so that they don't interfere with setting the gable truss. We adjust the gable truss to its positioning mark at the rear wall, then drive all of the nails we'd started earlier to fasten the bottom chord of the truss to the top plate of the end wall.

The strap holding the two regular trusses is then released, but the one holding the gable remains. We use a short length of 1x3 with the same 2-ft. layout as the wall plate to anchor the first two regular trusses to the gable. Then the bases are nailed to the wall plates on the rear wall.

Next, we brace the gable end with a couple of long diagonals running down to the

Spacers lock the peaks in position. One crew member holds the trusses in place while another attaches truss spacers (made by Truslock Inc.) along the peaks of the trusses. Strapping replaces the spacers so that only a couple of 16-ft. lengths of spacers are needed. The crew member at the rear of the house taps the truss into position on the wall plate and nails it home.

subfloor. The extra crew member then slides two 2x braces through the webs of the regular trusses, and the top ends of the braces are nailed as high as possible to the gable-end truss. We make sure that the braces won't interfere with the bottom chord of the next truss we lift into place. We plumb the gable truss with a level and a straightedge, and when it's ready, the extra crew member fastens the braces to 2x blocks that have been nailed through the subfloor and into joists. Only after the braces have been nailed at both ends do we release the strap from the gable truss.

After the first trusses are set, we usually lift two trusses at a time using a hook that the crane operator had made. The rest of the trusses go up rather quickly. One of the two crew members working the center of the trusses holds the trusses while the other fastens the Truslock truss spacers (photo, facing page). These spacers unfold, gripping the next truss and holding it at the proper spacing in one simple motion.

The two crew members working the middle of the trusses set the pace of installation and direct the others. The crew member at the rear of the house continues to align the positioning mark on each truss with the inside of the rear wall and nails his end of the truss securely with three 16d nails. The crew member at the front of the house just traps his end of the truss with a couple of nails (photo, above). After all of the trusses are up, we restraighten the walls and nail the front ends of the trusses with three 16d nails.

The extra crew member follows the action, strapping the ridge of the trusses with the 16-ft. 1x3s and tacking diagonal braces to secure the trusses until sheathing goes on. After the ridge is strapped, the truss spacers can be removed and used further down the roof. The top of the other gable end is tacked until we can set the distance between gables to the same measurement as the overall length of the house.

The front of the truss is left loose. With the trusses secured at the rear of the house and the peaks locked together, the front of each truss is allowed to float until after all of the trusses are in place. The walls can then be restrung and straightened if necessary before the fronts are nailed permanently.

The garage trusses are a breeze by comparison. The first truss has been braced to the house wall. We just set the trusses the same as before and plumb the garage gable after the crane leaves.

Lifting the materials and setting the trusses for a 2,600-sq. ft. to 3,200-sq. ft. house with an attached garage generally takes us three to four hours. By the end of the day, we usually have the entire roof sheathed and our subfascias set with a crew of five or six. If for some reason we can't sheathe at least one side of the roof before we have to leave for the day, we put on plenty of diagonal bracing to secure the trusses in case the wind decides to kick up during the night.

Rick Arnold and Mike Guertin are *contributing editors to* Fine Homebuilding *and the authors of* Precision Framing, *published by The Taunton Press.*

Sources

Truslock Inc.
2176 Old Calvert
City Rd.
Calvert City, KY 42029
800-334-9689
www.truslock.com

Building Hip and Valley Roofs with Trusses

■ BY RICK ARNOLD AND MIKE GUERTIN

A few years and many roofs ago, a builder approached us about framing a two-story colonial-style house. He said that he wanted to try a truss system for the hip roof. We had used trusses for a lot of gable roofs, but we had never seen a hip done that way. When the trusses for the job were delivered, we just stood back and scratched our heads. It looked as if bunches of unrelated pieces had been strapped together in no particular order. The engineering plan looked like a map of some unfamiliar suburb.

Too smug to admit that we needed help, we muddled our way through, lifting each weird-looking truss up to the roof by hand and then moving each piece three or four times until we found the right spot to nail it. That roof is still in good shape after two hurricanes, and whenever we drive by the house, we chuckle at how much time and effort it took to put that roof together.

Our methods for assembling hip-and-valley truss systems have evolved a great deal since that first puzzled attempt. The biggest advance in our technique came when we described the process to our crane operator. He suggested assembling some of the trusses on the ground and lifting whole hip sections onto the house in one shot. It worked like a charm. Now we even sheathe the assemblies before they go up.

Building Hip Systems on the Ground Is Quicker and Safer

Before anything is assembled, we prep the hip-and-valley trusses much as we do standard trusses. We line them up in a stack on the ground and mark layout lines for the sheathing and strapping and for alignment

The hip goes up in one piece. Like a giant box kite on a string, an entire hip section is lifted to its home atop a two-story house.

on the walls. If necessary, we also restack the trusses that will be lifted individually by the crane to be sure they're in the proper order. We lay out the wall plates according to the truss plan (sidebar, p. 144) and write the number and designation for each truss at its layout point.

When framing hip roofs with trusses, we most often use a step-down hip truss system (drawing, p. 142). Trusses in this system have the same span as common trusses, but they're flat on top. The flat parts of the hip trusses become progressively wider and lower as the trusses step away from the last common truss to begin forming the hip. The lowest and widest hip truss, the hip-girder truss, supports a series of monotrusses, called jack trusses, that complete the roof. The hip-girder truss usually has a heavier bottom chord than the other hip trusses to accommodate the extra

> *When framing hip roofs with trusses, we most often use a step-down hip truss system.*

weight of the jack trusses and the metal hangers that hold the jacks. Generally, two girder trusses are nailed together and work in tandem for each hip system.

After the wall plates are laid out, we lay out a hip-girder truss while it is still lying flat on top of the pile. We begin our layout by locating the exact vertical center of the truss, top chord to bottom (drawing, facing page). First we locate the middle of the top flat chord of the truss. Then from the ends of the flat chord, we measure equal distances diagonally to the bottom chord.

Halfway between our diagonal marks is the midpoint of the bottom chord. The line between the midpoints is the vertical centerline.

From this centerline we can locate the position of the outermost jack trusses on both the top and bottom chords as indicated on our truss plans. A jack truss is a monotruss with a single top chord. There are three different types of jack trusses in a hip system: face jacks that are attached to the face of the hip-girder truss and that run perpendicular to it; king jacks that run diagonally from the

A Step-Down Hip Truss Roof System

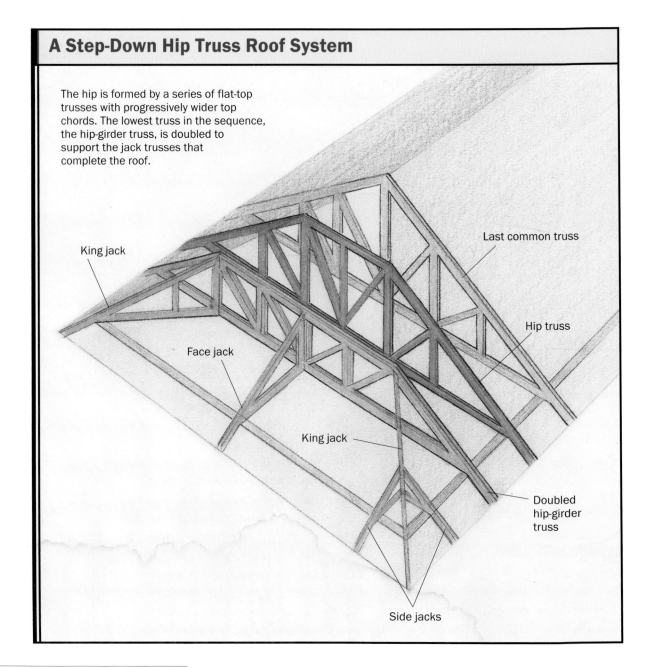

The hip is formed by a series of flat-top trusses with progressively wider top chords. The lowest truss in the sequence, the hip-girder truss, is doubled to support the jack trusses that complete the roof.

King jack

Face jack

King jack

Last common truss

Hip truss

Doubled hip-girder truss

Side jacks

Finding the Centerline of the Hip-Girder Truss

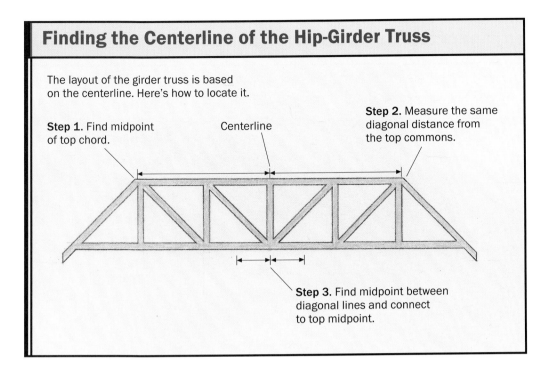

The layout of the girder truss is based on the centerline. Here's how to locate it.

Step 1. Find midpoint of top chord.

Centerline

Step 2. Measure the same diagonal distance from the top commons.

Step 3. Find midpoint between diagonal lines and connect to top midpoint.

girder truss and form the outside corners of the roof; and side jacks that are attached to both sides of king jack trusses.

The layout for the rest of the face jacks is taken from the wall-plate alignment mark on the girder truss. However, the center jack truss is always at the exact center of the girder, regardless of the spacing. We tack metal hangers for the face jack trusses onto the bottom chord of the girder truss with just a couple of nails in each hanger. They will be nailed in permanently with spikes after the second girder truss is mated to the first.

Jack Trusses Are Nailed to a Pair of Hip-Girder Trusses

Next we move the prepared hip-girder truss to a relatively flat area of the job site and prop it upright on blocks. The center face jack truss is set into its hanger and tacked to the girder truss at the top to hold them both upright (top left photo, p. 145). The tails of all of the jack trusses need to be supported, so we make a continuous block out of long lengths of 2x material. The blocking for the jacks is raised until the hip-girder truss is sitting fairly plumb, and the rest of the face jacks are then slipped into their hangers and tacked at the top. When they're all in place, we nail them off through the chords and webs of the girder truss.

Now we tack the second hip-girder truss to the first with just a few nails so that the girder trusses can be straightened before they are joined permanently. We run a stringline on the top and bottom chords of the girder trusses to get them straight. If need be, we temporarily brace the bottom chord against the ground to keep it straight (top right photo, p. 145). The tails of the face jacks are kept at the correct spacing with furring strips, marked to match the jack-truss layout and tacked on top of the bottom chords (bottom photo, p. 145). When the girder trusses are straight and the face jack trusses are spaced properly, we nail the two girder trusses together through all of the chords and webs, and we nail off the hangers for the face jacks.

We are now ready to square the assembly. First we recheck our strings on the girder trusses and then measure diagonally between

Truss Fabricators Engineer the Roof for You

Truss systems can be designed for almost any complicated roof design. Although the cost for the truss package may be more than the cost for conventional framing materials, the labor savings are phenomenal. As an added benefit, the interior bearing walls necessary for conventionally framed roofs can be eliminated, which allows greater design flexibility. Some of the truss packages we have ordered even include complicated details such as vaulted ceilings and roofs with hips and valleys of different pitches, roofs that would have been a real challenge to frame conventionally.

We've found that the best way to explore the possibilities is to go over the house plans with the engineer for the truss fabricator. At that meeting we often make arrangements for minor structural changes in the house to accommodate the roof trusses. Sometimes by moving a couple of bearing points or inserting a carrying beam, we can change a roof from conventional framing to a truss system. The benefits we gain by using trusses have always outweighed any changes we need to make.

After the meeting our fabricator usually gets back to us within a few days with a rendering of the truss plan and a price. We are occasionally astonished when a truss system ends up costing less than the lumber for a conventionally framed roof because trusses are made of less expensive, smaller dimension lumber.

We study the truss plan before the trusses arrive. If we're having trouble understanding a plan view of the system, the truss fabricator will provide an isometric drawing, usually at no extra cost. An isometric drawing shows the roof in 3-D and helps clarify the more difficult details.

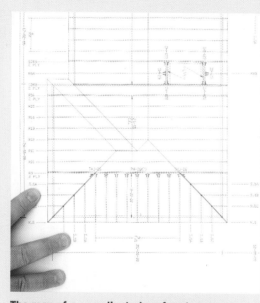

The map of a complicated roof system. Engineered-truss plans like this one are provided by the truss manufacturer. The plan identifies each type of truss and its exact location. This roof features a dozen different types of trusses.

the top chords of the two outermost face jack trusses (photo, p. 146). The tail ends of the face jacks are moved in unison until our measurements are equal and the face jacks are square with the girder truss. We check our strings one last time and nail a furring strip diagonally onto the underside of the top chords of the face jacks and on top of their bottom chords to keep the whole system square and uniform.

A 2x4 subfascia is now nailed to the tails of the face jack trusses and extended far enough to catch the tails of the king jack trusses when they're installed. We will straighten the subfascias after the hip systems are installed on the house walls. If the hip roof is going on a single-story house, we

A jack truss holds the girder truss upright. The center face jack truss is tacked to the girder truss to keep it vertical while the rest of the face jacks are installed.

Straightening the girder trusses. A temporary brace keeps the girder trusses straight while they are being nailed together.

A furring-strip spacer keeps the tails in place. Before the system can be squared, the tails of the face jack trusses are spaced according to the layout and held in position with a piece of 1x3.

Diagonal measurements square the system. Measurements are taken between the two outermost jack trusses, and the tails of the trusses are moved in unison until the measurements are equal.

For multistory houses we finish building the hip section on the ground.

ordinarily stop here. Because the staging is simpler for a single-story house and because materials can be passed to the roof directly from the ground, it's quicker for us to complete the assembly in place.

Special Hangers Hold the Jack Trusses for the Hip Corners

For multistory houses we finish building the hip section on the ground. The next step is tacking the king jack trusses in place (photo, facing page). The king jack truss is built with the top chord at the same pitch as a hip rafter and functions in much the same way. The king jack trusses are installed between

the hip-girder truss and the last face jack truss on both ends of the assembly. They fit into a specially designed hanger, provided by the truss manufacturer, that eliminates the need for the 45° angles normally cut on the top end of a hip rafter. We position the king jacks at exactly the same distance from the girder truss and the adjacent face jack truss, and we temporarily hold them in place with a furring-strip brace.

The tails of the hip trusses are usually left long by the manufacturer and cut to length on site. We run a string along the tails of the face jacks to determine where the tails of the king jacks need to be cut. We usually make this cut with a reciprocating saw because the subfascia tends to get in the way of a circular saw.

Next we cut the return angle on the tail of the first king jack. We find this cut by measuring along the bottom chord of the hip-girder truss from the first face jack truss to the end of the overhang. Then we measure that distance from the tail of the face jack to the tail of the king jack and make our cut there. The subfascia is cut to the same length and then nailed to the king-jack tail. On the other end of the assembly, we cut the king-jack tail and subfascia so that the length of the subfascia is the same as the overall length of the girder truss. The returning subfascias can now be nailed on. If possible, we extend the returning subfascias back beyond the girder trusses to tie in-

to the other step-down hip trusses when they are installed.

The side jack trusses are attached directly to the king jacks (photo, p. 148). A side jack truss is a simple monotruss with just a top and a bottom chord joined together with truss plates at the splice point. We locate the attaching points for side jacks by pulling 24-in. centers off adjacent girders and face jack trusses. The subfascias are laid out the same way.

Usually the manufacturer cuts the side jack trusses to the proper length but without the 45° angles on the ends of the chords. We cut these angles on site. For each hip system, there are four of each size side jack truss, two with right-hand 45° cuts and two

The tails of the hip trusses are usually left long by the manufacturer and cut to length on site.

The king jack truss forms the corner. The top chord of the king jack is cut to the pitch of a hip rafter and functions similarly. It is held in place with a special hanger, and the tail is positioned equidistant from the girder truss and the outermost face jack.

with left. Having one person organize and cut the side jacks minimizes the chances of cutting them wrong. Once the side jacks are cut with the proper angle, they can be positioned and nailed to the king jack truss and the subfascia.

We sheathe the trusses by snapping lines across all of the jack trusses and filling in as many sheets as we can. We don't sheathe return facets of the hips until the system is in place on the house so that our sheathing will tie back into the other trusses. Lower sheets are tacked in place temporarily so that we can lift them out of the way when we nail trusses to top plates.

Assembled Hip Sections Are Lifted Level

When we lift the hip sections, we run heavy-duty straps through the top corners of the hip-girder trusses where the king jack trusses are attached for the strongest lifting points (photo, p. 141). We attach an adjustable strap around the tails of the three middle face jack trusses to balance the load. The crane operator lifts the assembly just a little so that we can adjust the middle strap and get the assembly as level as possible before it's lifted into place. The more level the assembly is, the easier it is to position on the walls.

When the assembled hip system is airborne, a crew member stationed on the ground keeps it steady with a tag line until it is within reach of the crew on the staging. First we land the assembly at the layout marks on the plates for the hip-girder trusses. Then we have the crane tug the whole assembly toward the front or back until the lines on the bottom chord of the girders align with the inside edge of the walls. When the system is properly positioned, we release the straps and nail the trusses to the top plates of the end wall and along one side. The process is repeated for the opposite hip assembly.

The step-down hip trusses are now lifted into position one at time. We tack on short pieces of furring just below each of the flat sections to connect one truss to the next at the correct spacing. The process is repeated until we set the first full-height common truss. Then we pause the crane and tack a long piece of furring onto the flat tops of the trusses, measuring and spacing them properly as we go.

Side jacks fill in the framing beside the king jack. Side jack trusses consisting of just a top and bottom chord are nailed to the king jack and the subfascia.

The common trusses are sent up two at a time and locked in place temporarily with Truslock truss spacers. The layout for the last common truss is usually irregular to accommodate the step-down hip or valley system. We space that truss with a piece of furring marked to reflect the difference in the layout. The step-down hip trusses for the other end of the house can now be sent up one at a time and braced with furring as we did with the first end.

Building Valleys Out of Trusses Is a Snap

There are two basic ways of framing valleys with trusses. The one we encounter most frequently, and the easiest to frame, is the intersection of two simple roofs. We begin by setting all of the trusses for the main roof. If there are no interior bearing walls to support the trusses of the main roof where the two roofs meet, we hang the ends of the unsupported trusses on hangers nailed to a girder truss, which is part of the other intersecting roof.

Hips and Valleys next to Each Other Require Special Trusses

When a hip and a valley are too close together to be framed with conventional trusses, as in the drawing below, special step-down valley trusses have to be used.

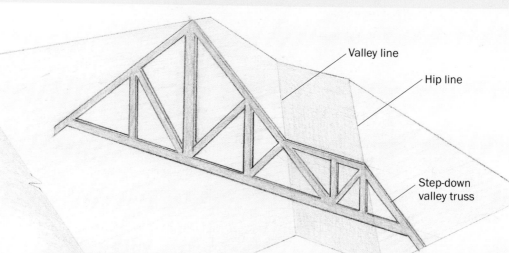

Valley line

Hip line

Step-down valley truss

Step-down valley trusses create the roof plane. When step-down valley trusses (photo, right) are installed, the flat portion of the top chord gets higher with each successive truss (photo, below), forming the roof plane between the hip and the valley.

Once the main roof has been sheathed, we set the trusses for the intersecting roof as far as the main roof. The valleys are created with a valley kit, which is a set of progressively smaller common trusses nailed directly onto the sheathing (photo, p. 149). We usually rip the pitch angle of the intersecting roof onto the bottom chord of each truss in the valley kit. Although cutting trusses is not a practice that is generally accepted, our truss manufacturer has assured us that ripping valley-kit trusses for this type of application is permissible.

If a valley is so close to a hip that a girder truss can't be used to hold the main roof trusses, a second method using special step-down valley trusses may be the answer (sidebar, facing page). These valley trusses are similar to common roof trusses except that the top chord is interrupted by a flat extension. The length of the flat extension is the same for every step-down valley truss and reflects the distance between the hip and valley lines. However, the height of the flat extension increases with each successive truss, creating both the valley and the hip as they go. Again, because each truss in the series is different, we take extra care to stack the trusses in the order that they will be lifted by the crane. Following the truss plan to the letter helps a great deal.

Reinforce Hip and Valley Lines with Blocking

After all of the trusses are set and the crane leaves, we complete the truss installation with a few extra details. First, we beef up the hips and valleys with 2x blocks cut with compound angles. These reinforcing blocks are not specified on the engineer's plan, but nailed between the step-down trusses at the hip and valley lines, they're helpful as spacers for the trusses and as nailers for the sheathing.

As with a simple truss roof, we nail the trusses only along one side of the house during the raising. After the crane leaves, we re-straighten the walls in case they've been knocked out of line while the trusses were set. When the walls are straight, we nail off the other end of the trusses. The rest of the subfascias can now be installed and shimmed straight. After our lunch break, we finish sheathing the roof.

Rick Arnold and Mike Guertin are contributing editors to Fine Homebuilding *and the authors of* Precision Framing, *published by The Taunton Press.*

Sources

Truslock Inc.
2176 Old Calvert City Rd.
Calvert City, KY 42029
800-334-9689
www.truslock.com

CREDITS

The articles compiled in this book appeared in the following issues of *Fine Homebuilding*:

p. 4: A Different Approach to Rafter Layout by John Carroll, issue 115. Photos by Steve Culpepper, courtesy *Fine Homebuilding,* © The Taunton Press, Inc. Illustrations by Dan Thornton, © The Taunton Press, Inc.

p. 16: Framing a Gable Roof by Larry Haun, issue 60. Photo on p. 21 by Eric Haun; all other photos by Robert Wedemeyer. Illustrations by Michael Mandarano, © The Taunton Press, Inc.

p. 28: Framing a Hip Roof by Larry Haun, issue 98. Photos by Larry Hammerness. Illustrations by Christopher Clapp, © The Taunton Press, Inc.

p. 38: Ceiling Joists for a Hip Roof by Larry Haun, issue 69. Photos by Susan Kahn. Framing models by Linden Frederick.

p. 42: Framing a Dutch Roof by Larry Haun, issue 93. Photos by Scott Gibson, courtesy *Fine Homebuilding,* © The Taunton Press, Inc. Illustrations by Bob Goodfellow, © The Taunton Press, Inc.

p. 49: Joining Unequally Pitched Roofs by George Nash, issue 68. Illustration on p. 55 by Bob Goodfellow, © The Taunton Press, Inc.; all other illustrations by Christopher Clapp, © The Taunton Press, Inc.

p. 58: Simplified Valley Framing by Larry Haun, issue 79. Photos by Larry Hammerness. Illustrations by © Mike Hiotakis.

p. 66: Framing a Bay Window with Irregular Hips by Don Dunkley, issue 57. Photos by Charles Miller, courtesy *Fine Homebuilding,* © The Taunton Press, Inc. Illustrations by Michael Mandarano, © The Taunton Press, Inc.

p. 78: Shed-Dormer Retrofit by Scott McBride, issue 35. Photo on p. 84 by Scott McBride. Illustrations by Chuck Lockhart, © The Taunton Press, Inc.

p. 88: Raising an Eyebrow by James Docker, issue 65. Photo on p. 89 by Charles Miller, courtesy *Fine Homebuilding,* © The Taunton Press, Inc.; all other photos by James Docker. Illustrations by Christopher Clapp, © The Taunton Press, Inc.

p. 96: Framing a Bay-Window Roof by Scott McBride, issue 129. Photo on p. 97 by Scott McBride. Illustrations by Christopher Clapp, © The Taunton Press, Inc..

p. 104: Framing an Elegant Dormer by John Spier, issue 130. Photos by Roe A. Osborn, courtesy *Fine Homebuilding,* © The Taunton Press, Inc. Illustrations by Christopher Clapp, © The Taunton Press, Inc.

p. 116: A Gable-Dormer Retrofit by Scott McBride, issue 134. Photos by Scott McBride. Illustrations by Christopher Clapp, © The Taunton Press, Inc.

p. 128: Raising Roof Trusses by Rick Arnold and Mike Guertin, issue 99. Photos on p. 131 by Scott Phillips, courtesy *Fine Homebuilding,* © The Taunton Press, Inc.; all other photos by Roe A. Osborn, courtesy *Fine Homebuilding,* © The Taunton Press, Inc.

p. 140: Building Hip and Valley Roofs with Trusses by Rick Arnold and Mike Guertin, issue 100. Photo on p. 149 by Mike Guertin; all other photos by Roe A. Osborn, courtesy *Fine Homebuilding,* © The Taunton Press, Inc. Plan on p. 144 courtesy of Trussco Inc., Davisville, R.I. Illustrations by Chuck Lockhart, © The Taunton Press, Inc.

INDEX